"I cannot imagine that any church serious about Jesus, his gospel, and his Word could not make excellent use of this short book that engagingly articulates old 'ministry values' in fresh and memorable ways. Don't be satisfied with one copy; buy a box of them and distribute them widely." (from the Foreword)

D. A. Carson, Research Professor of New Testament at Trinity Evangelical Divinity School, and President of The Gospel Coalition

"It is often said that gospel truth is not merely the means for conversion but is also a shaping power for all Christian life and ministry. But such a statement is often followed by generalities. Richard Coekin has developed a robustly biblical and eminently practical handbook for applying the gospel to the ministry of the local church. I recommend it!"

Timothy Keller, Founder of Redeemer Presbyterian Church, New York City, and President of City to City

"I have the highest possible regard, and gratitude to God, for the work of Co-Mission so faithfully led by Richard Coekin over these recent years. This book contains not only a faithful and masterful exposition of Acts 20 but also numerous helpful insights on gospel churches and Christian leadership from one who has been greatly used by God in our generation. It will be a most useful study for church leaders and leadership teams. I recommend it wholeheartedly."

William Taylor, Rector of St Helen's Bishopsgate, London

"One of our great needs is to have our hearts attuned to the heart of God. Richard's book, "Gospel DNA", serves this need wonderfully. And it does this by going straight to a passage rich with the themes and values of a gospel heart: Acts 20. The book is clear and easy to grasp, but deeply profound in its simplicity—and hugely practical and useful. A book to read and share."

Andrew Heard, Senior Minister, EV Church, and founding Director of "Geneva Push" church-planting network

"Richard Coekin's biblically rich, Christ-centred insights will encourage you to bolder evangelism, greater care for the integrity of the church and more careful exposition of the Scriptures. Be warned, this little book may inspire you to plant a church as the gospel's DNA replicates itself in your community."

Dr. Peter A. Lillback, President, Westminster Theological Seminary, Philadelphia

"A gem of a book which takes us back to the heart of gospel ministry—compelling us to keep teaching God's Word, pastoring his flock, seeking the lost and standing firm for biblical truth in a hostile culture. Immensely practical, biblically insightful, very humbling, and packed with helpful, personal examples. Brilliant!"

Paul Dale, Senior Pastor, Church by the Bridge, Sydney

"I am glad to commend this book. It's short, accessible and readable. It's faithful to the text, helpful in its application and honest in its assessments. It's from a particular context but it speaks to a wider audience. Richard has served us all well in writing it."

Steve Timmis, Global Executive Director, Acts 29

"There can be no better teacher on Christian discipleship, ministry and church-planting than the apostle Paul. And I can't think of anyone who could do a better job of applying his principles to today than Richard Coekin. I highly recommend this book."

Vaughan Roberts, Rector of St Ebbe's Oxford and Director of the Proclamation Trust

"This book is an ideal resource to help church leaders and church leadership teams re-evaluate their vision, programme and ministries. The immense gospel need in the UK today would perhaps begin to be addressed if every local church in the country were to reflect the gospel DNA outlined in this book."

John Stevens, National Director, Fellowship of Independent Evangelical Churches

GOSPEL
DNA

21 MINISTRY VALUES FOR
GROWING CHURCHES

RICHARD COEKIN

For my dear brothers and sisters in Christ
in all the congregations of the Co-Mission
church-planting movement, with love and gratitude
for our partnership in gospel ministry

"Whatever happens, conduct yourselves in a manner worthy
of the gospel of Christ. Then, whether I come and see you
or only hear about you in my absence, I will know that you
stand firm in the one Spirit, striving together as one for the
faith of the gospel without being frightened in any way by
those who oppose you." Philippians 1:27-28

Gospel DNA
© Richard Coekin/The Good Book Company, 2017

Published by
The Good Book Company
Tel (UK): 0333 123 0880. International: +44 (0) 208 942 0880
Email: info@thegoodbook.co.uk

Websites:
North America: www.thegoodbook.com
UK: www.thegoodbook.co.uk
Australia: www.thegoodbook.com.au
New Zealand: www.thegoodbook.co.nz

ISBN: 9781784980894

Design by André Parker. Printed in the UK

Contents

Foreword

D. A. Carson

Most Christians living in the UK who are interested in church planting will have heard of Richard Coekin and Co-Mission. My hope is that the publication of *Gospel DNA* will introduce this fledgling but seminal movement to many people in the US, as well as being of great service to those in the UK who wish to learn from the principles that underpin this growing church network.

Beginning with one small London church, Richard and those he has gathered around him for training and church planting have so far seen about thirty churches spring up, in London and its suburbs, with the aim of seeing another thirty planted by 2025, and (please God) 360 a little further down the road. One of the great wonders of Co-Mission, which provides the ministry structure for the movement, is its diversity: it includes people with posh backgrounds and Oxbridge degrees, and people with blue-collar backgrounds and sketchy education, and quite a lot in between. Similarly, these thirty churches reach out to very diverse segments of London's colorful and varied demographics. When a large percentage of these church members gather together for a weekend conference in June each year under the banner *Revive*, one of the startling (and hugely enjoyable) features of the assembled crowd is how diverse and unpretentious it is.

As he looks to the future, Richard is the first to acknowledge two things: first, there is no certainty—certainly no biblical promise—that the growth goals will be met; second, that by the standards of some rapidly expanding ministries in other parts of the world, the reach of Co-Mission still belongs to a day of small things—though in terms of reaching secular Londoners, the results so far are wonderfully encouraging.

This is not the place to outline the ways in which Richard fosters theological formation, or to explore the mentoring systems he has put in place, or to reflect on their use of strategic retreats for the church planters, and much else besides. One of the things that no observer can miss, however, is the effort of everyone in the movement to bring everything to the test of Scripture, and to become unreservedly loyal to a robust grasp of the gospel—what an older generation of evangelicals would have called adherence to a combination of the formal (Scripture) and material (gospel) principles.

One way in which this is distilled into the minds and hearts of new converts and church planters alike is through sharing the principles that you will find in *Gospel DNA*. This book is less an exposition of Acts 20:17-38, Paul's address to the Ephesian Elders, than a meditation on the passage—a meditation that distills twenty-one "ministry values" that surface in the text. These Richard casts as imperatives. Some of them are predictable—for example, "Teach the Bible because God is speaking its words today," or "Seek repentance and faith because anything less isn't salvation." Others are more tantalizing—for instance, "Accept unavoidable risk because God is sovereign," "Preach the kingdom because the best is yet to come," "Warn about judgment because we want to be innocent of blood," "Tell the whole truth because a distorted gospel doesn't save," and "Trust God because he is utterly magnificent." Co-Mission wants to see this "Gospel DNA" shaping all its churches, all its converts, all its church planters.

I cannot imagine that any church serious about Jesus, his gospel, and his Word could not make excellent use of this short book that engagingly articulates old "ministry values" in fresh and memorable ways. Don't be satisfied with one copy, buy a box of them and distribute them widely.

D. A. Carson
Research Professor of New Testament,
Trinity Evangelical Divinity School, Illinois;
President of The Gospel Coalition

Preface

Gospel DNA explores an electrifying training seminar for church leaders in Acts 20. It was delivered by an utterly extraordinary man of God—the evangelising, church-planting missionary Apostle Paul. This seminar not only offers unique insights into how Paul launched and strengthened multiple ministries in diverse contexts across first-century Turkey and Greece; it also clarifies God's foundational principles for effective gospel ministry in every age—with some radical challenges to the way we do church today! God has given us DNA in our bodies to carry genetic information that multiplies our distinctive physical characteristics, such as brown eyes or red hair, in our biological families. He has given us the "Gospel DNA" in this passage to multiply his distinctive spiritual characteristics in his church families. This book clarifies God's Gospel DNA, revealed in the Apostle Paul's sensational gospel ministry, for our churches today. Moreover...

Gospel DNA describes how these gospel-ministry principles have been applied in the churches of Co-Mission—an exciting church-planting movement that God is growing in London, UK. Named after Christ's "Great Commission" to make disciples of all nations, we were formed in 2005. From one small congregation in a school hall, God has grown us and enabled us to pioneer and establish about thirty new churches and ministries: some in the suburbs and some in the city centre, some working with urban elites and others in deprived housing estates or ethnic communities; others still are missions—to business people in Mayfair, homeless people in Victoria, and government workers and Members of Parliament in Westminster. Our emerging strategic plan is to plant thirty more churches by 2025, and our big hairy "360 Vision" is to launch 360 Reformed evangelical churches for London for Christ. God hasn't promised this—we may well fail! But we don't want to die wondering—so we're having a go. The growth we've witnessed, modest compared with some parts of God's global mission, but dramatic for a secular city like London, has been generated by God through ministries massively shaped by the Apostle's seminar in this passage in Acts 20. Indeed, much of the material in this book derives from the year-long ministry-training course that I have developed over the last 25 years, and through which so many Co-Mission pastors and planters have been trained. So this book clarifies what we pray is not only Paul's DNA, but also our Co-Mission DNA.

Gospel DNA is not a commentary or exposition. Rather, it identifies the major ministry themes as Paul mentions them, and explores what we learn elsewhere in Scripture about them—like descending in a hotel lift and getting out at each floor to explore a little. So *Gospel DNA* is for:

- **everyone** because it provides principles for gospel ministry in every age.
- **church leaders** because it clarifies foundations for apostolic church ministry.

This book is therefore ideal for ministry-training courses and leadership teams. Enjoy!

Richard Coekin
Director of Co-Mission, London
April 2017

Acts 20:17-38

[17] From Miletus, Paul sent to Ephesus for the elders of the church. [18] When they arrived, he said to them: "You know how I lived the whole time I was with you, from the first day I came into the province of Asia. [19] I served the Lord with great humility and with tears and in the midst of severe testing by the plots of my Jewish opponents. [20] You know that I have not hesitated to preach anything that would be helpful to you but have taught you publicly and from house to house. [21] I have declared to both Jews and Greeks that they must turn to God in repentance and have faith in our Lord Jesus.

[22] "And now, compelled by the Spirit, I am going to Jerusalem, not knowing what will happen to me there. [23] I only know that in every city the Holy Spirit warns me that prison and hardships are facing me. [24] However, I consider my life worth nothing to me; my only aim is to finish the race and complete the task the Lord Jesus has given me—the task of testifying to the good news of God's grace.

²⁵ "Now I know that none of you among whom I have gone about preaching the kingdom will ever see me again. ²⁶ Therefore, I declare to you today that I am innocent of the blood of any of you. ²⁷ For I have not hesitated to proclaim to you the whole will of God. ²⁸ Keep watch over yourselves and all the flock of which the Holy Spirit has made you overseers. Be shepherds of the church of God, which he bought with his own blood. ²⁹ I know that after I leave, savage wolves will come in among you and will not spare the flock. ³⁰ Even from your own number men will arise and distort the truth in order to draw away disciples after them. ³¹ So be on your guard! Remember that for three years I never stopped warning each of you night and day with tears.

³² "Now I commit you to God and to the word of his grace, which can build you up and give you an inheritance among all those who are sanctified. ³³ I have not coveted anyone's silver or gold or clothing. ³⁴ You yourselves know that these hands of mine have supplied my own needs and the needs of my companions. ³⁵ In everything I did, I showed you that by this kind of hard work we must help the weak, remembering the words the Lord Jesus himself said: 'It is more blessed to give than to receive.'"

³⁶ When Paul had finished speaking, he knelt down with all of them and prayed. ³⁷ They all wept as they embraced him and kissed him. ³⁸ What grieved them most was his statement that they would never see his face again. Then they accompanied him to the ship.

1. Learning from a legend

why Paul's teaching in Acts 20 is so precious today

Many centuries ago, I played rugby. One unforgettable highlight was when Clive Woodward, the hugely talented England player and future England coach, came to supervise a training session. I recall that he didn't do anything complicated. He took us right back to the fundamental principles of passing and tackling, and it was utterly electric. Especially because he was showing us how to do what we would watch him doing on television, scoring sensational tries for England.

It's the same in Acts 20. Paul was an original Apostle—authorised by the risen Christ to proclaim the gospel for him to the nations (Acts 9:15). He was also the heroic missionary, evangelist, church-planter and pastor. The man was a legend! And here in this passage we read of him training some local church leaders from Ephesus (a cosmopolitan regional capital city on the west coast of Turkey) by taking them back to the essentials of gospel ministry. Nothing complicated. He just explains what he'd been doing among them and on all his missionary journeys.

Here are three reasons why this sparkling passage should continue to have a formative influence upon us and our churches today:

First, this passage is a unique example of Paul's leadership training. The book of Acts is the second volume of a carefully researched history written by Luke. It describes what Jesus continued to do after his resurrection, by his Holy Spirit empowering his Apostles to proclaim the gospel "to the ends of the earth" (Acts 1:8). In this mission to the nations, it's often missed that Paul didn't only travel round Turkey and Greece evangelising and church planting. He also returned to the churches he'd started, "strengthening the disciples" (Acts 14:21-22; 15:41).

Luke includes various examples in Acts of Paul's evangelistic teaching, but this passage in Acts 20 is his unique example of how Paul strengthened the churches—by coaching their leaders in gospel ministry, so they could then train the members of the church. This was the way the churches could keep growing and multiplying with his "apostolic" gospel ministry at their core. Luke gives us a brief but brilliant summary of this momentous leadership seminar. He's clearly using Paul's own colourful phraseology, so that we can hear his coaching for ourselves. Since this passage is so special in Scripture, it remains precious to us today.

Second, in God's sovereign grace, Paul intentionally reflects upon aspects of his own gospel ministry that should be a pattern for future generations, and Luke recognises this by recording it. In this seminar, he focuses on three areas of his ministry that were not restricted to his special role as an Apostle but are for all generations:

- Proclaiming the gospel (v 20-27)
- Guarding the church (v 28-31)
- Providing the Word (v 32-35)

And in each section, he reminds them of how he'd already done what he's now telling them to do:

> "You know how I lived ... Remember that for three years I ...
> In everything I did, I showed you..."   Acts 20:18, 31, 35

Paul was plainly urging church leaders then and now to follow his example. We're not learning from a pompous, church-growth guru playing with radical theories in his comfortable university study! We're learning directly from Christ's missionary Apostle, who'd done it all before and carried the scars to prove it. Since these are the words of God, we must all listen and learn; since these are also the words of an Apostle who intends leaders to follow his example, our leaders must be ready to change. This teaching was clearly intended to shape the gospel ministry of church leaders everywhere and always!

Third, this training material remains particularly relevant today because it's not restricted to Paul's particular historical context. The heart of Paul's church-growth strategy for every culture was essentially the same: *Bible-teaching!* Indeed, in just a few verses he makes several references to its centrality in his ministry to them:

> "preach ... taught ... declared ... testifying ... preaching ...
> proclaim..."   Acts 20:20-27

And the silence about other aspects of ministry is stunning! This was clearly not a summary of his whole theology, so there are many important doctrines left unmentioned. But it was a summary of his foundational gospel-ministry themes and principles.

Luke records nothing about any strategies, staff teams or events he found useful. Indeed, there's nothing about community service, nothing about sacraments and nothing about useful cultural apologetics. In fact, we don't even hear anything about *how* to evangelise or *how* to plant or *how* to preach—much of which would have been specific to Paul's context. We know from the New Testament that these things were important to Paul, and presumably he did discuss these things with the Ephesian Elders that day (after all, what we do read here wouldn't have taken long to say!). But they're plainly not timeless essentials to be included here by Luke.

This is not an excuse for us to neglect the hard work of clarifying organisational strategies, cultural apologetics and expository preaching patterns for our own generation. Leaders with oversight of local churches must attend to these. But Luke is concerned here with Paul's training in foundational biblical themes and principles, and not with the widely varying strategies, skills and ministry cultures that we'll need to build upon them to be effective in different contexts today.

So these themes and principles will not be the whole of a leader's ministry. But they should be the foundations of all we do! The Co-Mission network I serve has planted in a wide variety of cultural contexts across London, each new church needing a very different strategic approach to evangelising their communities. But at the heart of all these strategies we must retain a commitment to the biblical themes and principles that Paul commends in this passage. The Apostle clearly intended them to be foundational for healthy local church life in every generation and culture.

Because these themes are so important, you will find that this book does not simply expound the verses here. Rather, in each verse, as we encounter a theme that is expanded on elsewhere in Scripture, we will briefly visit other parts of the Bible to understand that theme more deeply. After all, healthy biblical theology always interprets any part of Scripture in the light of the whole. You could say that, like descending in a lift from the top to the bottom of the passage, we will get out on every floor to have a little look around, in order to grasp something of the beauty of the whole building—which is faithful gospel ministry.

Finally, it is worth recognising in approaching this text that the cornerstone of these foundational ministry themes, whether in first-century Ephesus or twenty-first-century London, is "the good news (gospel) of God's grace". Paul says his life is completely surrendered to "testifying to the good news of God's grace", and he is happy to entrust the Ephesian church to "the word of his grace, which can build you up" (v 24, 32). Any teaching ministry that God uses to save people and grow churches today, whether in Tokyo, Melbourne, Rome, Montreal or London, will be devoted to believing and proclaiming the gospel of God's grace—his stunning kindness towards us in Christ.

We shall see later how this gospel is all about Jesus Christ, our loving Saviour and living Lord. If a local church is the body of Christ, and the Bible is its heart, then "the good news of God's grace" is the life-giving blood being continually pumped through the arteries of the various teaching ministries into all the organs and limbs of the church.

My prayer for anyone reading this book is that as you learn from the Apostle Paul, you will rejoice to discover, not only his foundational themes and principles for effective gospel ministry, but the lifeblood of that ministry in "the good news of God's grace", which saves sinners and builds churches today.

Think it through

1. What kinds of church ministry are you currently involved in? What would you say were their primary purpose and character?

2. Which church leaders / authors have had the greatest influence on your understanding of how to serve God in the past? How do you feel about learning from the Apostle Paul in Acts 20?

3. Write down below what you think are the most important elements of a local church ministry—that is, what do you think church leaders and members should primarily be involved in week by week? After you have finished reading this book, you could come back to reflect on this list and see whether studying Paul's teaching in Acts 20 has changed your view of church ministry.

Church leaders: How can you ensure that the gospel of God's grace is central in your church?

2. Train leaders

to equip God's people for ministries to grow the church

"From Miletus, Paul sent to Ephesus for the elders of the church." Acts 20:17

Paul was in a tearing hurry. He wanted to get to Jerusalem with a significant financial gift from the Greek churches for the poor Jewish believers. From there he planned to go via Rome to Spain, to begin a new mission (Acts 19:21; Romans 15). He was what you might call relentless for Jesus! But he couldn't bear to sail down the west coast of Turkey and ignore the Ephesian church that he'd planted and pastored, and which was now so vital to gospel work in the region.

Presumably, he dared not go into Ephesus and risk being captured by the authorities or delayed by the welcome of the church. So he stopped in the nearby port of Miletus, and sent for the church leaders to join him. One can imagine them arriving on mules and in horse-drawn carts, joyfully embracing their beloved Apostle and excitedly sharing news of families and friends.

Perhaps they gathered on a shaded taverna rooftop, swapping stories and chatting excitedly over a jovial meal, before settling down to listen intently to Paul's teaching. As Jesus had done with his disciples, so he was now training the next generation of church leaders so that, after his departure, the gospel message would continue to spread.

We would do well to learn from this. Too many healthy gospel ministries last only one generation. Churches sometimes decline or depart from the gospel after a pastor who has been faithful and fruitful for a season has paid insufficient attention to training up leaders from the next generation, or has neglected to carefully coach those who would appoint his successor. This involves not only clarifying the biblical theology and godly character to look for, but strengthening their determination and preparing their tactics to refuse inadequate leadership. No gospel ministry is truly complete until its succession is secured.

Paul trained leaders to train God's people in their ministries

Why did Paul train these Elders? In his glorious letter to their Ephesian church, Paul explains that Bible-teachers are given by Christ to train the people of God with the Word of God for ministries that will grow churches in spiritual unity and maturity in Christ: "to equip his people for works of service [ministry], so that the body of Christ may be built up" (Ephesians 4:11-13). This principle has had a massive influence upon our churches in London.

If we compare church to a soccer stadium, many people think of church like a crowd of spectators (the congregation) gathering to be entertained by incredibly expensive professional footballers (the clergy) playing the game (doing their clerical ministry). But Paul says that Bible-teachers are given by Christ "to equip his people", that is, it is the ministry of *all* Christ's people that builds up churches in number, unity and maturity.

To continue the soccer analogy, the teams of players (those who serve) are not just the clergy but all the believers. They are led by their captains ("Elders" leading by their teaching and example) and trained by their player-coaches (the preachers and small-group leaders) with the coaching manual (Scripture). They play the game (loving God, loving each other and loving their community) and nurture the youth academy (teaching Scripture to the children) against the opposition (sin, the world and the devil). The watching crowds are unbelieving friends, family, work colleagues and local community. Our "ministry teams" should therefore include *all* the believers in our congregations. (Unbelievers in church can be included in practical service, but not in teaching or singing what they don't believe; and it's unwise to give unbelievers a ministry that may give them the impression that they're saved, which will cause them to drift away when their imitation faith doesn't work.)

Notice that Bible-teaching is training—and training for everyone. Paul doesn't restrict this to potential pastors, or even ministry leaders. If the church is grown by God through the ministry of all the members, then all the members will benefit from biblical training to ensure that their ministry is done in a godly manner and is connected to the common cause of making disciples. Paul presumably not only coached his Elders in how to train small-group leaders, children's workers and song-writers in careful Bible-handling, but also coached them in how to offer appropriate Bible-teaching to train those with less celebrated ministries, like visiting, befriending, bringing, welcoming, hospitality and conversational ministries. As all the instruments in an orchestra have an important role in creating beautiful music, the ministries of all the church members combine in growing the church. Paul's church-growth strategy is essentially training people with the Bible for their diverse "body-building" ministries—so every church is a "training church" and every member of it needs "ministry training".

It's worth recognising that practical operational ministries must serve the spiritual ministries of growing disciples of all nations for Christ. We certainly shouldn't despise strategic planning, operational support, or buildings and aesthetics—they provide platforms for Word ministries. Sadly, churches can so despise these ministries that their spiritual growth plateaus unnecessarily. There is much to be gained in reaching the lost from the wise, strategic planning that is integral to the role of Elders, who oversee, or manage, the household of God (for example, consider developing "purpose-driven" ministry teams rather than simply multiplying clergy).

However, we must remember that strategy, planning and operations exist to serve the collective purpose of making disciples of all nations for Christ. To borrow an analogy from Marshall and Payne's brilliant book, *The Trellis and the Vine*, the supporting organisational structures of the church (the trellis) *only exist* to serve the spiritual growth of the church (the vine). Sadly, churches can become so consumed by exciting, new church-management systems and building schemes that they neglect to teach and train people deeply with the Bible, and wonder why the congregation remains immature and unwilling to serve. The trellis supports the vine and not vice versa. Elders need to ensure that strategies and structures are effective in supporting the training of God's people with God's Word in their ministries—to grow God's church in number and in Christ-like unity and maturity.

Paul trained the "Elders"

In this passage God provides a priceless "executive summary" of Paul's training for church Elders. This term, "Elders", means "senior men". We know that the Apostle required Elders for the spiritual health of every church, and regarded a church without appointed Elders as incomplete. It was for this reason that he left Titus in Crete to appoint for every planted church Elders who were morally "blameless" and doctrinally "sound" (see Titus 1:5-9).

"Elders" are to be plural, a team that benefits from different gifts, experience and energy (not a one-man band). They are to be spiritually senior (not inexperienced youngsters), to benefit from the experience, wisdom and authority that come with maturity. And they are to be men, because every church is God's family, needing men to provide loving leadership (in 1 Timothy 2, Paul explains why from creation).

Paul elsewhere says that Elders must be marked by personal godliness, Bible-teaching ability and a capacity for overseeing the congregation. They are not to be self-appointed but chosen by other senior leaders, and publicly commissioned (ordained) to be recognised by other churches and their own congregations as having God-given authority as "overseers" (literally, "presbyters" or "bishops"—who supervise and manage) and "shepherds" (who lead, protect and provide) in their local church.

Many churches (including ours) explicitly appoint a group of Elders. In other churches that don't explicitly do this, there will often be leaders who *function* as Elders (for example, in Anglican and other Episcopal churches it may be the rector and wardens). It is normally vital for the health of a church to identify and authorise those who will function as Elders, in order to exercise the vital ministries that Paul is about to explain. Without them, the church cannot readily grow to spiritual maturity.

How a team of Elders functions in practice will vary enormously by culture and tradition. In some cultures, churches may confer great authority upon their employed Elders (especially those recognised or ordained as presbyters or bishops by their denomination). This enables them to lead proactively, but can lead to apathy in the congregation and pride in the leaders. In other cultures, churches may develop more democratic leadership. This may encourage the involvement of church members, but can constrict the proactivity of the leadership and may lead to tensions in the church or inertia in the leaders.

Ideally, churches will incorporate the best of both worlds, encouraging church members to recognise the godliness and gifting of their Elders and staff, allowing them plenty of blue-sky freedom to initiate progress without expecting the congregation to be consulted in every decision; but also encouraging employed staff to value the godly wisdom and multi-disciplinary skills of mature church members and gladly to accept accountability to their team of Elders (or a senior group of them sometimes called "Governing Elders").

Healthy churches will have Elders and staff who *both* exercise proactive leadership *and* wisely recognise occasions when it is necessary to patiently consult the congregations. It may also be worth observing that it is generally advisable to establish a constitution, create governance structures and clarify terms of employment for staff when the church is happy and growing, rather than naively assume that such things will never be necessary and regret the lack of clarity when conflict arises.

Paul knew that to train the whole church in their body-building ministries would first require training the Elders.

And not just training *them* to do the ministry, but training them to train *others* in it—not just *adding* gospel ministers but *multiplying* gospel ministers.

While Elders will benefit from studying these ministry principles themselves, it's helpful if they can be sufficiently self-aware to recognise where they are weak and need to recruit help, whether from inside or outside the church. For example, I have needed help both from other Elders and younger colleagues with professional management experience in learning to manage staff teams and develop appropriate operational support for our church as it grew larger. (The article *Leadership and Church Size Dynamics* by Tim Keller and the book *Ready, Steady, Grow* by Ray Evans are hugely helpful in understanding how significantly the size of a church affects its ministries.)

Indeed, I have recently asked a senior pastor whom I greatly respect from another church to be my informal "coach". For if there's anything to learn from the world of sport, it must be the value of coaching. A junior-school team might have one coach, a club team might have several, but the national team will have dozens of coaching staff for every aspect of play! Yet in church life, the more senior we become, the less training we often receive. Generally speaking, senior Pastors and Elders can have the greatest influence for spiritual good in a church, but if they fail, theologically, morally or emotionally, can cause enormous damage. May I encourage senior church leaders continually to *seek* coaching as well as to *offer* it (whether more curriculum-driven training from colleges and conferences, or more issue-driven mentoring from a more senior minister)?

We need to learn Paul's priority commitment to providing biblical training for those who will train God's people in their ministries that grow the church.

Think it through

1. What Bible-training have you received for the church ministries you are involved in?

2. What strategies are there in your church for identifying and training the next generation of pastors / evangelists / church-planters / missionaries / financial patrons / small-group leaders / women's workers / children's workers? What about more low-key ministries like bringing and hospitality?

Church leaders: *How could you improve the quality of the training you provide? And how could you arrange for the training that you need?*

3. Share your life

because gospel ministry is caught as well as taught

"When they arrived, he said to them: 'You know how I lived the whole time I was with you, from the first day I came into the province of Asia.'" Acts 20:18

Gospel ministry is a way of life

As the Ephesian leaders settled down to listen to their beloved Apostle, it's very striking that he started by commending "how I lived". Paul doesn't say, "You know what I taught" and then recommend his latest epistle for detailed study. He wants the Ephesian leaders to recall and imitate his lifestyle because gospel ministry is a way of life. Yes, the gospel message itself is verbal. It must be carefully studied and learned from the Bible. But an effective and enduring gospel ministry that will proclaim that gospel in many different contexts is a way of life shaped by the gospel and dedicated to proclaiming it in diverse situations.

And sharing that lifestyle with less experienced leaders is the best way to train them in it, because they witness an integrated lifestyle that is sustainable in multiple settings. For example, no college curriculum can possibly tell you what to say... to your wife when she feels neglected because of your church commitments, to your gay hairdresser who wants your approval of his lifestyle, to your daughter when she comes home having split from her boyfriend, to your church colleague who proposes training as a missionary to Rwanda, to your youth group needing help with being holy among friends exploring city nightclubs, or to a congregation wanting to evangelise hostile colleagues in their secular workplaces. But a gospel-shaped person has something sensible to say in all of these contexts because they know how to work from gospel principles to practical realities.

Gospel ministry is not just a set of intellectual concepts or professional skills to be learned from a commentary on Ephesians or a leadership seminar. Books and lectures can certainly be helpful, but gospel ministry is a pattern of life moulded by the gospel.

Bible-teaching was plainly the heart but not the whole of Paul's gospel ministry. In some church contexts, leaders need to be reminded of the centrality of Bible-teaching: that Sunday expositions of the Bible, mid-week small-group Bible discussions, and one-to-one biblical mentoring should be the first priority of the church leader's ministry. In these churches, learning better skills in text-interpretation is urgently needed, because it is "the word of his grace, which can build you up and give you an inheritance among all those who are sanctified" (v 32).

However, in other churches, the preacher is spending long hours in the study polishing intellectually excellent sermons for a tiny group of people that aren't growing. In particular, no one is training leaders to train the people in gospel ministry by sharing a gospel-shaped life with them. And any training that is provided is entirely conceptual and theological. Please don't misunderstand me here—biblical theology is the basis of everything in church life. So the one evening course that I have always run throughout every year for the last 25 years has been my "Prepared to Serve" applied theology course for potential leaders. But courses are not enough on their own to train ministers. Sadly, leaders trained in an exclusively academic environment, without any practical mentoring such as is experienced, say, as a ministry trainee (or "apprentice") or as an assistant minister (or "curate"), often struggle to cope with the messy pressures of church life. They have no experience of practical patterns of ministry to fall back on.

Paul was plainly committed to the most rigorous theological study, but only as the heart of a broader training in gospel-ministry lifestyle. Paul reminds these leaders confidently: "You know how I *lived* [literally 'was' or 'became']"—he knew that healthy patterns of gospel ministry are as much "caught" as "taught". And so, as Jesus had trained his disciples by taking them with him on his unforgettable missions around Israel, and as Paul trained bands of co-workers by taking them with him on his dramatic missionary journeys around Eastern Europe, so he had shared his life with these men in Ephesus to train them in local-church gospel ministry. We can learn from this approach, not only when we get to train leaders, but from our first opportunities to evangelise and pastor church members. Not that Paul expected to be able to share life with all the church members once the church had grown beyond this being practical—but he's reminding leaders to train others to share their lives with others.

Gospel ministry is best learned from sharing life

Paul elsewhere summarises this pattern of coaching disciples by sharing life in parental terms:

> "Just as a nursing mother cares for her children, so we
> cared for you. Because we loved you so much, we were
> delighted to share with you not only the gospel of God
> but our lives as well."   1 Thessalonians 2:7-8

This commitment to personal mentoring by sharing life has been evident in many kinds of gospel-ministry training: as "apprenticeships", developed in Australia by Jensen and Marshall, and in the UK (including our Co-Mission churches) with the encouragement of the 9:38 ministries (named after Jesus' command to pray for more workers in the Lord's harvest, in Matthew 9:38), and in the US as "internships". Indeed, most of our Co-Mission churches have been planted and staffed by former Apprentices/Interns, who now coach their own ministry trainees, who in turn share life with those they are seeking to disciple.

The aim is that these men and women share not only in learning Reformed evangelical Bible doctrine, but in an effective lifestyle of gospel ministry. This pattern of ministry is our church-family likeness, multiplied among our various church plants—our "gospel DNA" (hence the title of this book). The foundations of this lifestyle must be biblical principles, such as are outlined in Acts 20. But on these foundations we must also then build effective patterns of ministry for the different cultures we work in.

In London, our ministry DNA includes pioneering, can-do team work, commitment to cultural diversity, and a passion for biblical training to multiply (not just replicate) workers. Other contexts may need to develop a different set of emphases. My point is just that there is more to an effective ministry culture than sound foundational theology. There are many Reformed churches that are theologically sound but have ineffective patterns of ministry. Paul was eager to remind the Ephesian

Elders not just of the theological principles that we have in Acts 20, but of his whole lifestyle, which was built on them. Indeed, Paul will remind Timothy of this again, when urging him to be loyal to his pattern of suffering for the gospel of the cross:

> "You, however, know all about my teaching, my way
> of life, my purpose, faith, patience, love, endurance,
> persecutions, sufferings ... continue in what you have
> learned."   2 Timothy 3:10-11, 14

A key ingredient of effective gospel-ministry training will therefore be the trainee sharing in the life of a more experienced pastor, with personal coaching in *head* (knowledge of Scripture), *heart* (Christ-like character) and *hands* (gospel-ministry skills), which develops confidence in sustainable as well as sacrificial patterns of biblical ministry.

What a joy it's been to me over the years to share life with so many godly men (and their families) who are now the senior pastors of Co-Mission. It felt entirely appropriate to ask my first three Apprentices to be godparents to my son because they are so dear to my family (though they still owe me for some pizzas they ordered and left me to pay for one Saturday night when they came round to watch football!) Indeed, the warm co-operation of our network is built upon the mutual trust and affection of senior pastors who learned gospel ministry together by sharing a gospel way of life that is built on biblical foundations. This is what Paul was reminding his Ephesian Elders about.

Gospel ministry will adapt to different cultural contexts

Notice that Paul describes his way of life "the whole time I was with you". He's speaking about his unchanging essential ministry principles rather than the various adaptations he made for ministry in different cultural contexts, becoming "all things to all people so that by all possible means I might save some" (1 Corinthians 9:22). There is an important clarification to make here.

It is imperative to be flexible in cultural aspects of ministry. Paul even had Timothy circumcised to avoid culturally offending the Jews! I'm very much in agreement with those who observe that churches are often unaware of how their ministry culture can alienate unbelievers from different cultures. We must try to ensure that the way we do our church ministries is culturally as accessible as possible for the communities we're trying to reach. Some will express anxiety about shaping church for any particular culture because the gospel is for all nations and heaven will be wonderfully multicultural. However, since every church does inevitably develop its own particular culture, it's preferable to be intentional about this and consciously try to adapt to the community we're aiming to reach rather than be naively alienating them.

Integration is a *process* not a *moment*

Like many other Western cities, London is wonderfully multi-cultural—and we are trying to make disciples of all nations right here in London. But these cultures are often socially segregated by numerous cultural and historical factors. So if we want to reach into these communities, we need to shape or "contextualise" our *ministries* to be accessible to them. Over time we can then disciple those who are converted to enjoy the glorious diversity of God's people as we prepare to live together in heaven. Throughout Co-Mission we're committed to a radical flexibility of culture and to contextualising our *ministries* appropriately; for example, the ministry of our churches in deprived housing estates is intentionally very different to that of our churches working with privileged, young urban elites, and both are very different to our churches working in ethnic communities or among suburban families. Paul championed cultural flexibility.

However, we must also be faithfully *inflexible* in preaching the unchanging gospel of Christ.

Gospel ministry should not contextualise the gospel itself

While we gladly contextualise our ministries (including the shape of our teaching programmes), we are uncomfortable when talking of contextualising the gospel itself.

One of the most powerful proofs of the truth of the gospel is that the same gospel of our Lord Jesus Christ is believed by churches all over the world. In order to thrive, Islam needs an Arabic culture, Buddhism needs an East-Asian culture, Hinduism needs a South-Asian culture, and atheism needs a Western culture. But the same gospel of God's grace in Christ is enjoyed by Christians in every culture.

Certainly, different aspects of the same gospel will be more appreciated or more provocative in different contexts. But it is our joyful experience that our dear friends among Palestinian Muslim-background believers in Jerusalem and among Belarusian communist-background believers in Minsk and among animist-background believers in rural Rwanda believe the same gospel, and live by the same Bible, as our Westernised brothers and sisters in Sydney, New York, Cape Town and London. We may have very different music, but we sing the same words.

We may start in different places in teaching this gospel in different communities, but we need to arrive at the same destinations in God's gospel regarding Jesus Christ our Lord (see chapter 9). In Acts 20, Paul is recommending, for all future generations across all the cultures of our planet, some unchanging ministry principles which were foundational to his own gospel-ministry lifestyle. Church leaders everywhere need training in this lifestyle so they can share it with others!

Think it through

1. *Why do you think it's important for leaders to share their lives with those they want to train?*

2. *Would your church leaders encourage you to find a coach or to be a coach in gospel ministry?*

3. *What would it mean for your church to contextualise its gospel ministry effectively for the unbelievers of your community? How would you shape an outreach service differently for your work colleagues, your neighbours or your family—and what would remain the same in them all?*

Church leaders: *How could you arrange for you and other mature believers in your church to "share life" to some degree with those who could fruitfully learn gospel ministry from you?*

4. Serve the Lord

whatever the cost, because you worship him

"I served the Lord with great humility and with tears and in the midst of severe testing by the plots of my Jewish opponents." Acts 20:19

We've all heard of the brutal indignity of slavery in the ancient world. Yet Paul often gladly described himself as a "servant" (also translated as "slave" or "minister") of our Lord Jesus. Although he was once a highly respected religious scholar, Paul had been bought with the blood of Christ. He now belonged to Jesus and had absolutely no rights of his own.

In this, he was clearly following the example of Jesus, who said:

> "Whoever wants to become great among you must be your servant, and whoever wants to be first must be slave of all. For even the Son of Man did not come to be served, but to serve, and to give his life as a ransom for many." Mark 10:43-45

So Paul introduces himself in his letters as, "Paul, a servant of Christ Jesus" and called upon others to live as slaves of Jesus— "keep your spiritual fervour, serving the Lord" (Romans 1:1; 12:11). Gospel "ministry" is slavery to Jesus the Slave!

Serving the Lord is worship

Yet this language of ministry and slavery is also the language of "worship". The Bible describes worship in three dimensions— adoring reverence, humble submission and obedient service of God. And our ministry is not a reluctant performance of a tyrant's demands but a welcome opportunity to worship our beloved Saviour. As followers of Jesus, our highest ambition is to hear his words of approval on the day of judgment: "Well done, good and faithful *servant!*" (Matthew 25:21).

Serving the Lord is personal

Some Christian cultures talk primarily of being ministers of the gospel, some of being ministers of grace, some of being ministers of the Word and some of being ministers of the Lord. All are biblical. The Apostle chooses here to emphasise his personal submission to our Lord.

It's right to say that we're servants of *the gospel* so that our ministry isn't superficial. Most non-Christians believe something superficial about Jesus—that he lived or preached or did miracles. But these truths won't save anyone. To be saved we must believe some important particulars about Jesus that are declared in God's gospel regarding him: that Jesus (the crucified Galilean) is the Christ (the promised Saviour-King), our Lord (the divine and risen ruler), who came as our King, died for our sins, rose to rule and will return to judge. Paul warned, "By this gospel you are saved ... Otherwise, you have believed in vain" (1 Corinthians 15:1-8, see chapter 9). So we are certainly servants of the gospel. However...

We should also emphasise that we're servants of *grace* so that our ministry doesn't become a religious performance. Gospel ministry is not about God's work *in* us, but about God's work *for* us in Christ. Too often, we who know we *become* justified by faith in Christ's ministry for us slip into assuming that we *stay* justified by our ministry for him! Without an emphasis upon God's grace, we will become either proud of what we achieve or terrified when we fail. We need constantly to recall that we are servants of the gospel... of grace. However...

We must also emphasise that we are servants of *the Word* so that our ministry doesn't become culturally shaped and politically correct. If we don't deepen our understanding of the gospel of grace with what God says in his Word, we'll be tempted to promise all the politically-correct benefits that our culture wants us to promise, such as financial prosperity, sexual freedom or forgiveness without repentance. We need to keep reforming our understanding of the gospel with God's Word so that it isn't twisted by our cultural preferences. We are servants of the gospel... of grace... in God's Word. However...

We must also emphasise that we are servants *of the Lord* so that our ministry doesn't become mechanistic and impersonal. We're not saved merely by understanding historical facts about Jesus, however biblical they are. In 18th-century Scotland, the followers of Robert Sandeman over-reacted to the emotionalism of their day by proclaiming salvation through "bare belief in bare truth". This movement, called Sandemanianism, was utterly dry and impersonally intellectual. Thankfully, a theologian called Andrew Fuller (among others) showed that genuine biblical faith includes personal delight in and joyful affection for the Jesus of the gospel. We must avoid becoming functionally Sandemanian in being so scornful of expressions of affection for Christ—in the name of resisting emotionalism but in reality out of cultural reserve—that we are actually suppressing the delight of genuine faith. After all, the demons know that Jesus is the Holy One of God (Mark 1:24) but remain unsaved because they have no faith in him that is affectionate or repentant—they neither love nor obey him. We want to be slaves and ministers of the gospel... of grace... in God's Word... regarding the Lord we love. Perhaps Paul chose to say, "I served the Lord" (Acts 20:19) because, deep in his heart, his ministry and worship were captive not just to the gospel programme, but to the gospel person: the Lord who bled and died for us.

Serving the Lord is often painful

When Paul says, "I served the Lord with great humility and with tears", he's not boasting that he's humble but admitting that he's been humiliated. There'll often be shame and hurt in gospel ministry. Tears of frustration when someone we've nurtured walks away from the Lord; tears of exhaustion when church members expect standards of performance we can't manage; tears of embarrassment when we've let people down. When God chose to love us, he voluntarily opened himself up to being hurt by us, ultimately on the cross—so when, like him, we love people in gospel ministry, we open ourselves up to being hurt by them. Paul admitted, "I wrote to you out of great distress and anguish of heart and with many tears, not to grieve you but to let you know the depth of my love for you." (2 Corinthians 2:4). Serving the Lord will often be painful.

Serving the Lord is often opposed

Like Jesus before him, Paul faced continual opposition and plotting against his ministry, for example:

> "They stirred up persecution ... Jews who refused to believe stirred up the other Gentiles ... there was a plot afoot ... they stoned Paul and dragged him outside the city ... [the] Jews were jealous; so they rounded up some bad characters ... agitating the crowds and stirring them up ... some Jews had plotted against him."
>
> Acts, chapters 13 – 20

Notice that his chief opponents were religious leaders who were jealous of Paul's success and plotted to stir up state authorities against him (especially provoking the Roman powers to regard Christianity as a dangerous cult undermining the authority of Caesar, rather than the fulfilment of the ancient Jewish religion, which was tolerated in the empire). Not much has changed. The twin powers of state and religion (pictured in Revelation as "beasts" serving the dragon—Satan) will always tend to suppress Christianity, even though Jesus told Pilate, "My kingdom is not of this world" (John 18:36). Even in Western cultures with a Christianised heritage, loyalty to biblical teaching on sexual morality or gender difference, and gospel initiatives like church-planting and street-preaching are likely to face opposition from establishment religion and state ideology.

But Western churches shouldn't dwell with self-pity on such opposition, for three reasons.

First, this is normal. Paul wrote, "Everyone who wants to live a godly life in Christ Jesus will be persecuted" (2 Timothy 3:12).

Second, this is a privilege. Jesus said, "Blessed are you when people insult you, persecute you and falsely say all kinds of evil against you because of me. Rejoice and be glad, because great is your reward in heaven" (Matthew 5:11-12).

Third, our troubles are minor—at least, minor compared with the sufferings of many dear brothers and sisters (according to the Open Doors watchdog) in North Korea, Eritrea, Iraq, Afghanistan, Pakistan, Syria... A North Korean believer at our church recently drew my attention to distressing reports of Christians in North Korea being used in chemical experimentation, and their pastors laid down in a line while a steamroller crushed their heads in full view of their families. They certainly know what Paul, himself often beaten and stoned (2 Corinthians 11), means when he writes of "severe testing" (Acts 20:19). They will be wonderfully rewarded by our Lord in eternity, when he embraces each in turn and declares as promised, "Well done, good and faithful servant ... come and share your master's happiness!" (Matthew 25:23).

As Dietrich Bonhoeffer famously wrote from his Nazi prison, "Suffering, then, is the true badge of Christian discipleship. The servant is not above his master" (*The Cost of Discipleship*). All servants of *the* Servant must take up our cross if we want to inherit our crown.

Think it through

1. *How does it make you feel to be described as a "slave of Christ"?*

2. *What kind of opposition have you faced for following Jesus?*

3. *Take time to pray for your brothers and sisters around the world who face brutal persecution.*

Church leaders: *In what ways do you, or your church, find yourself tempted to pull back from proclaiming and contending for biblical faith for fear of unpopularity or opposition? Are there ways you have given in to those temptations? Do you need to repent?*

5. Teach the Bible

because God is speaking its words today

"You know that I have not hesitated to preach anything that would be helpful to you but have taught you publicly and from house to house." Acts 20:20

It's crystal clear from this passage and the rest of the New Testament that Paul evangelised, planted and built up congregations throughout Turkey and Greece by teaching the Bible! In just a few verses summarising his work among the Ephesians, we read of him preaching, teaching, declaring, testifying and proclaiming the word of God (Acts 20:20-27).

But it's a massive mistake to think this just meant Sunday sermons! Paul says he taught "publicly", evangelising unbelievers in the cauldron of the Jewish synagogue or among the jostling crowds of the city square. But he also taught privately, "from house to house", instructing believers in the Ephesian house churches, presumably in various ways: perhaps sermons on Sundays in the courtyard gatherings, Bible-study discussion groups mid-week after work, one-to-one discipleship and biblical counselling whenever possible. In a whole variety of ways, the Spirit of God grew the churches of God through the Word of God.

So today, the reasons that people give for joining healthy congregations in London include the experience of God addressing them personally through his Word. Even when the reasons are expressed in terms of a warm welcome, exciting children's ministry or compassionate outreach, it's important to realise that these things are the product of God transforming people through his Word.

Spiritual life comes only from the Spirit of the living God through his living Word. We'll consider the dynamic power and absolute authority of God's Word when we study "the word of his grace" in Acts 20:32. Here in this verse, Paul explains that God gives spiritual life through teaching ministries. Again, Paul isn't saying that Bible-teaching is the whole of Christian ministry, but he is saying that it's the heart of all Spirit-empowered church growth.

In Acts 20:27, Paul will recall that he never hesitated to teach "the whole will of God", including the politically incorrect bits of the Bible that no one wants to hear. But here he reminds his listeners that he also didn't hesitate to teach them whatever would be helpful for their spiritual development. He considered the condition and needs of the congregation as well as the variety of Scripture.

Paul's teaching programme combined the need to teach all of God's Word with the need to be sensitive to the particular age, maturity, challenges and opportunities of the people he was teaching and the cultural season in which they lived. This is why we generally benefit more from average teachers who know our spiritual condition than from beaming in a great preacher like John Piper on a screen. John's a better preacher than any of us in our church network, and we'll occasionally listen to his exceptional historical studies to great profit; but he can't possibly know the spiritual condition of our congregations in the way a local pastor will from week to week.

There are many ways to faithfully expound the Bible. As long as we listen to the text rather than using it for our own agenda, it's probably not helpful to speak of right and wrong ways to teach; so here are some ways we have found "helpful" in applying Paul's variegated approach in verses 18-27 to teaching in our London churches, remembering that we adapt our teaching styles considerably for different communities.

Our normal Sunday teaching is usually *expository* (explaining a Bible passage) rather than *topical* (collecting texts that deal with an issue from all over the Bible). This stems from a shared conviction that, although occasional topical talks are valuable for addressing particular subjects, expository preaching provides a more varied diet of God's Word in the form that he wrote it. This helps to avoid squeezing Scripture into our human theological systems and favourite tribal agendas. It also helps people learn how to understand the Bible for themselves, and encourages them to test what a preacher says by what they can see in their own Bibles.

Some of our Sunday congregations enjoy having short topical answers to current issues in the same gathering as a series of longer sermons expounding consecutive Bible texts. This helps to combine "anything that would be helpful" in addressing current issues with hearing "the whole will of God" in all of Scripture. Other churches offer these two kinds of teaching in different meetings; for example, consecutive texts (often those being preached on) will be discussed in mid-week small groups and then supplemented by an occasional series of evening seminars that consider pressing current issues or ministry skills.

But on Sundays we generally prefer the dangerously challenging experience of hearing whatever the living Spirit of our Lord will say to us as consecutive passages are expounded, rather than choosing for ourselves what message we think we should hear in a topical series. We're keen to listen and not misuse the Bible.

Four influences

Godly and able preachers vary in their approach to preaching and teaching (again, there's no "right" way to preach so long as we're explaining what God's Word says, and not using the Bible to endorse what we want to say!). In our network, there are hugely different personalities working in a wide variety of contexts with very different styles of preaching. But it may be helpful to identify four welcome influences upon us all:

First, most of us appreciate being influenced through **involvement with youth camps** by the teaching principles of John Stott (and Charles Simeon before him). This promotes an emphasis upon *allowing the structure and content of a Bible passage to provide the structure and content of our teaching.*

Second, most of us appreciate being influenced through the UK **preaching conferences of The Proclamation Trust** (and its Cornhill Training Course) by the teaching principles of Dick Lucas. His emphasis upon *understanding any Bible passage in the context of its book* has been massively important. He has urged our generation to carefully study the text to discern within it the main aim(s) of the author and the main theme(s) used to achieve that aim. A recurring theme being used for an evident aim helps to reveal the main message of a book, like the melodic line in a piece of music. Clarifying this main message can really help us interpret the supportive details throughout the book.

Third, most of us have appreciated being influenced by the **teaching principles of Australian preachers** such as John Chapman, Phillip Jensen and John Woodhouse to *use the whole Bible to interpret any part of the Bible*. This awareness of "biblical theology" is based on three simple principles:

1. Behind various human authors of the Bible books there's one divine editor, the Spirit of God; this means that the different books are consistent with each other and we can and must use different passages of Scripture to interpret each other.

2. Through various historical periods in the Bible there's one unfolding historical drama revealing the kingdom of God; this means we need to remember both the background and the outcome of any part of this overarching history.

3. Among various characters described in the Bible there's one central hero, the Son of God; so every verse is related to understanding salvation through him. Old Testament descriptions of judges, prophets, priests and kings, and institutions like the temple or the Sabbath, and the theology of redemption from slavery in Egypt, all contribute to helping us appreciate Jesus.

Fourth, most of us have been influenced more recently by the **teaching principles of the "Gospel Coalition" preachers** in the USA, especially Tim Keller, John Piper and Don Carson. In particular, their emphasis upon *careful application of the necessary implications of the Bible text to the lives of those in global urban cultures* has proved enormously helpful.

In all our teaching, we share a commitment to *clarity*. Paul wrote, "Pray that I may proclaim it [the gospel] clearly, as I should" (Colossians 4:4). The great evangelical leader J.C. Ryle once wrote with typically insightful colour, "I thought it my plain duty to *crucify my style*"; and it was said of that great 18th-century preacher George Whitfield, "Whitfield's preaching was singularly *lucid and simple*. His hearers, whatever they might think of his doctrine, could never fail to understand what he meant." Our Co-Mission preachers certainly all aspire to such clarity.

Above all, we share the conviction that the aim of Bible-teaching is to help people understand and respond to the words of God's Spirit in the text of Scripture with repentant faith.

For we delight to be governed by this written message from our wise Creator, awesome Judge, loving Saviour and providential Father. Prayerful Bible-teaching remains the heart of the ministry of Co-Mission churches in London and of every church willing to learn from the Apostle Paul's ministry, because it was the heart of the gospel ministry of our Lord, who said, "Let us go somewhere else—to the nearby villages—so that I can preach there also. That is why I have come"; and who then commanded his disciples, "Make disciples of all nations, baptising them in the name of the Father and of the Son and of the Holy Spirit, *and teaching them to obey everything I have commanded you.* And surely I am with you always, to the very end of the age" (Mark 1:38; Matthew 28:19-20).

Think it through

1. *"Anything that would be helpful to you" (Acts 20:20). On what particular issues and biblical themes do you think it is most important to teach in your church context?*

2. *What strategies have you found that help you get the most out of hearing Bible preaching? (For example: taking notes / returning to the passage next day / praying over the sermon at the end of church with someone else.)*

3. *What would you say distinguishes good from bad preaching?*

4. *What has God been teaching you recently as you have heard his Word preached?*

Church leaders: *Is the careful exposition of God's Word appropriately given its primary place in the ministries of your church and its staff?*

6. Seek repentance and faith

because anything less isn't salvation

"I have declared to both Jews and Greeks that they must turn to God in repentance and have faith in our Lord Jesus."

Acts 20:21

Here Paul recalls that the saving response that God sought and created through Paul's gospel teaching was not just intellectual comprehension or emotional stimulation, but repentance and faith. You can imagine the Elders murmuring at this point as they fondly remembered how challenging Paul's gospel had sounded at first—indeed, how offended the Jews in the synagogue had been to be told that they too needed to repent and believe. Paul faced their fury nearly everywhere he went.

Repentance and faith are actually two sides of the same coin. So sometimes we read of God requiring "repentance"; for example, to the Gentile intellectuals of Athens Paul says, "He commands all people everywhere to repent" (Acts 17:30). But on other occasions we see that God requires "faith" (the word can equally be translated "belief" or "trust"); for example, to the Philippian jailor, Paul says, "Believe in the Lord Jesus, and you will be saved" (Acts 16:31). This is because repentance and faith are twin aspects of turning around—turning *from* a life of sinning (repentance), which is turning *to* a life of trusting God (faith).

"Repentance" means turning from sin

The word translated "repent" means "change your mind". But this is deeper than intellectual assent. It means changing our mind to the depth of our will (what we intend to do) and our affection (what we love). That's why John the Baptist insists on repentance being expressed not just in words but in action: "Produce fruit in keeping with repentance" (Matthew 3:8).

It isn't saving repentance just to understand the gospel, feel the power of the gospel, agree with the truth of the gospel or even wish we could change because of the gospel! Repentance means changing our mind deeply enough to actually start behaving and loving differently, even though this may be costly. We can't promise to be perfect because our sinful nature remains in us. But real repentance means genuinely trying. Paul tells King Herod Agrippa, "I preached that they should repent and turn to God and demonstrate their repentance by their deeds" (Acts 26:20).

The Old Testament background to this idea of "repentance" is found in the words "sorrow" (for sin) and "turning" (from idols), which were characteristic of Old Testament prophets calling people back to the LORD, such as Elijah at Mount Carmel in a dramatic showdown with the prophets of Baal, where God was "turning" the hearts of the people from idols back to himself (1 Kings 18:37).

This duty to clearly teach a need for repentance in saving faith is one of the main factors that churches will bear in mind when choosing which evangelistic course to use. Many Reformed churches, including our Co-Mission churches, use the *Christianity Explored* courses because of the clear commitment to explaining simply the need to repent. This involves turning from our own way of sin to Christ's way of faith, from worshipping the idols of this world (when good things like wealth and comfort, career and status, pleasure and entertainment, family and security are worshipped as God even though they cannot satisfy and will not save) to worshipping God.

"Faith" means turning to trust God

The word translated here as "faith" is often translated "believe". It means to trust, rely or depend upon something or someone. When unbelievers say, "I wish I had your faith", they don't realise that they already exercise faith when they get on a train trusting it to take them somewhere, or when they take medicine prescribed by a doctor.

They do have faith, but not yet in Christ for salvation. Such faith in Christ is only created in spiritually dead unbelievers by the Holy Spirit through the gospel, for "faith comes from hearing the message" (Romans 10:17). But that doesn't mean that Christian faith is an irrational confidence in fantasy!

The gospel we believe is true and it is evidenced with copious proof in the Scriptures. There is overwhelming logic, impressively detailed prophetic predictions, miraculous signs and wonders, and multiple eye-witness accounts. That's why the method by which people come to salvation is not manipulation, which bypasses the mind, but persuasion, which addresses the mind. For example, Paul "reasoned with them from the Scriptures, explaining and proving ... arguing persuasively about the kingdom of God" (Acts 17:2-3; 19:8). However, when we were unbelievers, we were spiritually blinded by Satan to the facts that become obvious with faith.

This word "faith" is massive! It summarises:

- *our way of knowing God* (believing what he says about himself).
- *our way of salvation by God* (believing his gospel promise).
- *our way of pleasing God* (trusting his Word enough to obey him).
- *our way of experiencing God* (feeling the meaning of his words).
- *our way of serving God* (confident of his return).

When I first arrived to study for a year at Moore College in Sydney (I joke with my Australian friends that it generally takes Aussies four years, but one is enough for an Englishman!), the magnificent college principal, Peter Jensen, invited me for dinner. As we washed up the dishes, he asked me a searching question: "What word do you think best summarises the Christian life?"

I was utterly clueless. I squirmed around for what seemed like hours suggesting all sorts of ridiculous words until he finally put me out of my misery. "How about 'faith'?" he quietly suggested. I was humiliated, but have never forgotten that lesson.

Since God's saving initiative in Christ is applied to us through the words of the gospel, the word that best summarises the whole Christian life is indeed *faith* that receives that gospel. Our relationship with God will therefore always primarily be about him speaking through his personal Word (Christ) in his written Word (Scripture), and us responding in faith expressed in words of dependent prayer—a conversation in which he speaks through his Word and we respond by faith in prayer.

The New Testament also emphasises three things that faith is not

"Faith" does not require experience but trusts God's Word—"faith is confidence in what we hope for and assurance about what we do not see" (Hebrews 11:1). With countless Old Testament examples from Abraham through to the time of Jesus, we're reminded that faith enables believers to trust God's apparently impossible gospel promise enough to persevere through hardships for an unseen future. Saving faith does not demand to experience now what God has promised in his Word.

"Faith" is not works of obedience to the law—"we, too, have put our faith in Christ Jesus that we may be justified by faith in Christ and not by the works of the law" (Galatians 2:16). Romans and Galatians are especially clear that permanent salvation is by faith that trusts in the righteous obedience of Jesus that he lived for us, and not by the utterly inadequate works of our own lives. Saving faith trusts God to save us from start to finish.

"Faith" is not neglectful of good deeds—"faith by itself, if it is not accompanied by action, is dead" (James 2:17). James is not contradicting Paul, for Paul himself writes, "The only thing that counts is faith expressing itself though love" (Galatians 5:6). James and Paul both insist that real faith is expressed in behaviour. We are saved by Jesus' godly life of good deeds and not ours. However, we're saved by him for a life of good works. Real faith in Christ will always be expressed in good deeds towards others. These deeds aren't the reason why we're saved, but they are the result and evidence of being saved. Saving faith is expressed in good works of love.

In Paul's ministry, and in churches today that learn from him, repentance and faith are not only the two sides of that fundamental change of direction when we first turn from sin to Christ for salvation. Repentance and faith are also the continuing and characteristic response that God seeks in every area of our lives whenever we hear the Word of God. It's not that we are becoming Christians every time we repent and believe his Word. Rather, God's Spirit calls every aspect of our lives to become consistent with our new direction of life. Repentant faith is our Christian lifestyle!

Think it through

1. *What did repentance involve for you when you turned to follow Christ?*

2. *How do you, and how does your church, ensure that unbelievers understand that repentance is integral to becoming—and growing as—a Christian?*

3. *How would you answer an unbelieving friend who asked, "You say Christianity is a life of faith. What does that actually mean?"*

Church leaders: *In what ways is your church tempted to settle for something less or other than repentance and faith in its ministries?*

7. Accept unavoidable risk

because God is sovereign

"And now, compelled by the Spirit, I am going to Jerusalem, not knowing what will happen to me there." Acts 20:22

"Risk is right!" thundered the great American preacher John Piper in characteristically dramatic fashion at the start of his address to the Evangelical Ministries Assembly in London. Then for added effect he shouted again, even more loudly, "Risk is right!" He proceeded to give us examples from Scripture where people are commended for taking risks because they trusted God.

This verse from Acts 20 also illustrates that principle. Paul simply didn't know what would happen when he got to Jerusalem. Paul was no hothead, but sometimes we just can't know what will happen.

In obeying Christ's great commission to make disciples of all nations, sometimes we have to trust God and have a go. Rather than holding back and waiting until everything is sorted out and risk free, which will probably never happen, we can trust our loving heavenly Father because he's in control.

In our church-planting, we've sometimes accepted unavoidable risks, not because we're impetuous or think we'll manipulate God into doing what we want, but because we're convinced that God is looking after us. We try to minimise the risks as much as possible, but we still can't be certain how it will turn out. Sometimes a more cautious observer will suggest that the planting group seems too small or the financial support is too uncertain. Sometimes the buildings or locations aren't marvellous or the leadership isn't ideal. We know they're right and we may well fail, but we are willing to try our best and have a go.

We can't guarantee success. It's just that, since we're trying to obey Jesus in making disciples by planting churches, and since our loving Father is sovereign, we trust that he can employ our weakness for his glory and pick us up if we fall flat on our faces. For the biblical doctrine of the sovereignty of God is not just for technical argument about how salvation works. Trusting this truth creates an atmosphere in which we can be bold in mission, taking unavoidable risks because God is sovereign. Let me explain.

We believe that God controls everything

From prison, Paul reassured these Ephesians that God "works out everything in conformity with the purpose of his will" (Ephesians 1:11). Contrary to the lies of the "open theologians", God hasn't left anything to chance. He works everything together—including our sins, Satan's assaults and apparently random tragedies—for the good of those who love God, which God defines as becoming like Jesus (Romans 8:28-29). God is always perfectly accomplishing his plans even when we have no idea what they are. It's precisely because God is not taking any risks that we can. Since he's completely in control, we don't have to be. We don't have to know what will happen, because our heavenly Father does. This is part of what it means to live by faith in God!

We believe that God predestines, provides and preserves

As part of his universal sovereignty, God is also sovereign in the lives of individual people. This begins with his loving predestination of people for salvation. Paul wrote:

> "For [God] chose us in him [Christ] before the creation
> of the world to be holy and blameless in his sight. In
> love he predestined us for adoption to sonship through
> Jesus Christ, in accordance with his pleasure and will."
>
> Ephesians 1:4-5

God's election (choosing some but not all sinners for salvation) and predestination (deciding our future) are not cranky or cruel as many assume (indeed, Jesus clearly taught this doctrine in John 6:37-40).

Some worry that believing in predestination will make us *neglect evangelism* (because God will save people without us), *neglect holiness* (because we'll be saved however unholy we are) or *neglect humility* (because we'll feel superior). The opposite is true.

Election and predestination make us evangelise more because we know that God saves his elect and predestined people through evangelism (indeed, if God didn't choose to save some, there'd be no point in us even trying). Moreover, election and predestination encourage our holiness because, like happy children adopted into a privileged family, we try hard to please our new Dad. And election and predestination actually undermine arrogance because we discover that we're saved only by God's grace and not because we're superior.

So we can accept unavoidable risks in gospel ministry, such as planting churches without any certainty of success, precisely because God uses his people to find his *predestined* people scattered across the world. Our plans and churches don't have to be perfect, because God can use our weakness to magnify his power in saving his elect (2 Corinthians 4:7). We can accept unavoidable risks because God is sovereign in saving his chosen people.

God is also sovereign in his loving *provision* of our daily needs. Our heavenly Father delights to give us good gifts. Jesus said:

> "Do not worry ... why do you worry ... do not worry ... your heavenly Father knows that you need them. But seek first his kingdom and his righteousness, and all these things will be given to you as well. Therefore do not worry..."   Matthew 6:25-34

I don't think Jesus was excusing sloppy planning. And I don't believe that living by faith means we don't have to try hard to raise the resources of leaders, people and funding that we will need (compare Acts 20:34). But faith in our Father's loving providence does encourage us to work tirelessly and then trust that he'll provide what we really need. And he always has! We can accept unavoidable risks because our heavenly Father provides all we really need to do his work his way.

And God's sovereignty includes his loving *preservation* of his children all the way to heaven. Jesus promised that he'll lose no one who comes to him. How could anyone chosen before creation by God the Father, redeemed at the cross by God the Son, and sealed with the indwelling guarantee of God the Holy Spirit, ever be lost by God? God preserves us by both challenging and empowering us to persevere. For example, Paul writes, "Work out your salvation with fear and trembling, for it is God who works in you to will and to act in order to fulfil his good purpose" (Philippians 2:12-13).

God preserves us by keeping us persevering. We don't know that our plants will all grow, but we do know that God will keep us persevering. Trusting his loving preservation encourages us to take unavoidable risks and keep trying! Nothing unexpected or undesired by God for our good can ever happen—for God is preserving us.

So God's sovereignty allows us to be opportunistic and entrepreneurial. We can't hope to plan everything in advance, because we are only human. But, in every opportunity, we recognise God's sovereign hand. In his parable of the talents, or bags of gold (Matthew 25:14-30), Jesus likens himself to a master who entrusts resources to his servants while he's away. When he returns, he commends two servants with the words, "Well done, good and faithful servant!", because they made the most of what they'd been given. The third servant is condemned because he just protected what he had. He didn't take any risk in trying to do something creative with the master's resources. This infuriates the master.

Jesus was warning that many will be horrified to discover that attempting nothing for Jesus reveals that they were never his true disciples—because genuine disciples care so much for their Master's gospel business that they will accept unavoidable risks to advance it. Real disciples don't live too safely, because they love their Master enough to have a go.

"Let's see what happens if..."
Across Co-Mission we're trying to have a go, though we don't know what will happen. I recall one godly wife of a staff

member asking me some years ago what our ten-year plan was. I felt rather inadequate as I admitted, "Well, I don't really have a ten-year plan. I thought we'd preach the gospel and try very hard and see what happens." That was enough for a while. Now that our movement has grown and gathered momentum, we do have a ten-year plan for planting sixty churches; we have a leadership team and some strategies and resources; but beyond this, we still have no idea what will happen. We are still having to accept many considerable and unavoidable risks and we may well fail. But we are going to have a go and not die wondering! Just like the Apostle Paul, we don't know what will happen, but "risk is right"... because God is sovereign!

Think it through

1. *How does the thought that God is sovereign over every area of life make you feel? How should it make you feel?*

2. *When was the last time you took a real risk for God? What particular fears tend to stop you from doing so?*

3. *How would your life be different if you were absolutely convinced that God is in control and generously provides all that we need?*

Church leaders: *Is there an unwillingness to accept unavoidable risk in the mission of your church and its people? How would understanding the sovereignty of God affect this?*

8. Enjoy the Holy Spirit

because he's working powerfully among us

"I only know that in every city the Holy Spirit warns me..."
Acts 20:23

In all of our Co-Mission churches, you'll find an open appreciation of the ministry of God the Holy Spirit, the third person of the divine Trinity. Put simply, if God the Father planned our salvation and God the Son accomplished our salvation, then God the Holy Spirit applies our salvation to our experience.

Jesus said, "He will glorify me" (John 16:14). Professor J.I. Packer describes this fundamental aspect of the Spirit's work as his "spotlight ministry". I once saw a wonderful sound and light show at the Blue Mosque in Istanbul. An incredible array of spotlights lit up the magnificent main dome, six minarets and eight minor domes. The spotlights were not there to draw attention to themselves, but to the magnificence of the building. Likewise, the ministry of the Holy Spirit is to draw attention to the magnificence of Jesus, rather than to himself. Churches and individuals in whom Jesus is glorified are churches and individuals that are full of the Holy Spirit.

Speaking for a moment specifically of our Co-Mission churches in London, we wouldn't describe ourselves as "charismatic", because we don't expect prophetic messages from God outside the Bible. We trust that "the Spirit of truth" guided the Apostles into "all the truth" to give us everything we need to know in God's Word, as the unique "light shining in a dark place", that we may be "thoroughly equipped for every good work" (John 16:13; 2 Peter 1:19; 2 Timothy 3:17). But again, we wouldn't describe ourselves as "cessationist", because we believe Scripture teaches that God continues giving his gifts of grace to his people for serving others with love (1 Corinthians 12 – 14). We need and celebrate the ministry of the Holy Spirit in our lives and churches.

But what is that ministry? In appreciating the Holy Spirit, it's important to consider the whole of biblical teaching, because an unbalanced concentration upon selected passages often leads to distortion and unnecessary division. There is naturally a variety of views among evangelicals concerning secondary issues of the Spirit's ministry, but most will celebrate the following blessings of his presence.

The Old Testament celebrates the Spirit's ministry in creation, renewal and leadership

In the Old Testament, God created faith in his people by his Holy Spirit through his gospel promise to Abraham. But his Spirit didn't yet indwell believers as he has since Christ's ascension. Nevertheless, there were three glorious aspects to the Spirit's ministry:

- **Empowering creation:** Reflecting upon the co-operation of God's Spirit and Word in creation, we read, "by the word of the LORD the heavens were made ... by the breath [Spirit] of his mouth" (Psalm 33:6). Just as our breath carries out our words when we speak, the breath of God—his Holy Spirit—empowered his words in creation. This explains our new creation when we become Christians. Jesus told Nicodemus that we must be "born of the Spirit" but Peter says, "You have been born again ... through the living and enduring word of God" (John 3:3; 1 Peter 1:23). The Spirit of God created the universe and now recreates his people through his Word.

- **Empowering renewal:** The Old Testament promised that God's Holy Spirit will renew God's people; for example, "I will give you a new heart and put a new spirit in you" (Ezekiel 36:26). To illustrate this, Ezekiel was given a famous vision of a valley of dry bones, full of skeletons, representing the spiritual deadness of Israel. Indeed, we all live in such valleys today. Sydney, Tokyo, Cairo, Rio and London may be full of social and intellectual life, but spiritually are filled with millions of dead people—skeletons in valleys of death. Ezekiel was told to declare God's Word and then pray for the breath, or Spirit, of God. By God's Word and Spirit together, the skeletons came to life, illustrating the future in which we now live, when the renewing power of the Spirit brings people alive through the gospel. Churches everywhere are full of regenerated skeletons!

- **Empowering leadership:** The Holy Spirit empowered prophets to speak, kings to rule, judges to rescue and artists to create for God. They all pointed to the promised

Messiah; for example, "The Spirit of the LORD will rest on him—the Spirit of wisdom and of understanding" (Isaiah 11:2). So when Jesus came, "the Holy Spirit descended on him ... Jesus, full of the Holy Spirit ... led by the Spirit into the wilderness ... Jesus returned to Galilee in the power of the Spirit" (Luke 3 – 4). As promised, Jesus was empowered in his human nature for all his ministries by the Holy Spirit. (Of course, his divine nature needed no help from anyone.)

The New Testament celebrates various aspects of the ministry of the Holy Spirit, but they are all related to Christ:

The Spirit taught the truth about Christ

At his farewell meal, Jesus taught lots about his Holy Spirit. He promised, "I will ask the Father, and he will give you another advocate ... the Spirit of Truth ... will teach you all things and will remind you of everything I have said to you" (John 14). So the Spirit continues the "advocate" ministry (or teaching) of Jesus through the Apostles' writing in the New Testament. Notice that he will "remind" *them* of what Jesus taught them—and not us, who weren't there. He continued, "He will prove the world to be in the wrong about sin and righteousness and judgment" (John 16:8); that is, the Spirit will testify to Jesus through his Word to convict us of our sinful lack of righteousness to survive the day of judgment, and of it being provided for us in Christ.

The Spirit enables all God's people to prophesy about Christ

In Acts 2, as promised in the Old Testament and by Jesus, God poured out his Holy Spirit upon his disciples to renew them. This was evident in them boldly proclaiming "the wonders of God" done by Jesus in the languages of many nations, as promised to Abraham. Empowered by the Holy Spirit, Peter then preached an evangelistic sermon by expounding Old Testament passages to show that Jesus is the promised Messiah. Peter explains from Joel that the Spirit now enables all God's people to prophesy, proclaiming what the Bible says about the wonders of God done in Jesus. All of God's people can prophesy about Jesus in this general way ("for it is the Spirit of prophecy who bears testimony to Jesus", Revelation 19:10).

The Holy Spirit gives new life in Christ

In a most glorious exploration of our new life in the Spirit (Romans 8), the Apostle proclaims that the Holy Spirit brings us...

- **New government:** "The mind governed by the Spirit" through his Word (Romans 8:6).

- **New life:** "The Spirit gives life ... life to your mortal bodies because of his Spirit" (Romans 8:10-11), for the Spirit who raised Jesus has raised our spirits to life now and one day will raise our bodies also.

- **New battles:** "If by the Spirit you put to death the misdeeds of the body, you will live. For those who are led by the Spirit of God are the children of God" (Romans 8:13-14), so the Holy Spirit empowers us to kill or "mortify" our sinful nature (and this is being "led by the Spirit").

- **A new Father:** "The Spirit you received brought about your adoption to sonship. And by him we cry, '*Abba*, Father.' The Spirit himself testifies with our spirit that we are God's children" (Romans 8:15-17), for the Spirit of the Son convinces us of the gospel, that by faith in him we are also sons of God entitled to pray to our loving heavenly Father.

The Holy Spirit is the seal and deposit of life in the presence of Christ

Paul reassures the Ephesians that "when you believed, you were marked in him with a seal, the promised Holy Spirit, who is a deposit guaranteeing our inheritance" (Ephesians 1:13-14). The presence of the Holy Spirit in our lives seals and guarantees our salvation because God has taken up permanent residence in us. Indeed, his indwelling gives us a foretaste or "deposit" of our inheritance, which is life in his presence. He indwells us individually and corporately in all our churches as a "temple of the Holy Spirit" (1 Corinthians 3:16-17; 6:19; 2 Corinthians 6:16) to bless us with just the first course of the feast in heaven.

The fruit of the Holy Spirit in our lives is Christ-likeness

Paul explains that holiness comes from "living by the Spirit" (Galatians 5:13-18). This isn't walking around hearing messages or tingling with miraculous powers. It means being willing and able to serve one another in love. Perfection is impossible in this life, because our sinful nature remains until we get to heaven. But the Spirit creates in us an internal conflict with our own selfishness. The Spirit daily calls us to the holiness of "the fruit of the Spirit", a growing and beautiful Christ-likeness with nine virtues of love, joy, peace, forbearance, kindness, goodness, faithfulness, gentleness and self-control (Galatians 5:22-23).

The Spirit gives us all gifts for serving the body of Christ

The New Testament rejoices that Christ gives all his people "grace-gifts" (*charismata*) for serving the church through building each other up in their faith in Christ (1 Corinthians 12 – 14). There are all sorts of gifts. Some are more remarkable, like healing—others less remarkable, like administration. None of us are given all the gifts; we may have many or few, and develop or lose them as God determines.

Most gifts are clearly a competence to do very well what most Christians can only do averagely—like encouragement or helping. But whether our gifts are many or few, ordinary or spectacular, all of us are needed in the church. We are like limbs united in Christ's body, each with special and complementary gifts to contribute. So no one should feel unnecessary or superior. We're all different: like musicians in an orchestra, we're all valuable and all necessary for playing beautiful music. To the Corinthians, over-excited by the gift of "tongues" (ecstatic language), Paul says this gift is only for personal benefit unless interpreted, and is therefore less valuable in church than prophecy.

Prophecy is a gift to be more highly valued because it should edify people in the faith. The prophecies in Corinth were clearly spontaneous revelations (presumably insights into Scripture) from God. This doesn't mean that prophecy is receiving messages in addition to Scripture. The gift of prophecy seems to be a God-given ability to contribute fresh insights into Scripture, such as you will hear every week in Bible studies or in discussing a Sunday sermon. We should weigh and value, rather than treat with contempt, such prophetic insights into God's Word. The biggest challenge of 1 Corinthians 14 is not to look for messages from God beyond Scripture (which we can't expect), but to welcome the prophetic gifts of church members offering their God-given insights into his Word (which we can expect).

All these aspects of the ministry of God the Holy Spirit are evident and appreciated in Reformed churches like ours. We are being filled with the Holy Spirit (Ephesians 5:18) as his Word fills our lives (Colossians 3:16) to enable us (as explained in the passages just reviewed) to understand the truth about Christ, prophesy the gospel about Christ, experience new life in Christ, enjoy a deposit of the presence of Christ, grow in the holiness of Christ and lovingly serve the body of Christ. We are, spiritually, skeletons brought to life to know Christ and serve his people, by the Holy Spirit through his Word. Praise God for the glorious ministries of his Spirit in our lives and our churches!

Think it through

1. *In the light of what you have just read, what does it mean for an individual or church to be "Spirit-filled"?*

2. *Which aspects of the Spirit's ministry are most evident in your church?*

3. *Which parts of the Spirit's ministry have you most failed to appreciate?*

Church leaders: *Which aspects of the Holy Spirit's ministry described above are understood and celebrated in your church and which are not? How can this be rectified?*

9. Proclaim the gospel

because it reveals the grace of God

"I consider my life worth nothing to me; my only aim is to finish the race and complete the task the Lord Jesus has given me—the task of testifying to the good news [gospel] of God's grace." Acts 20:24

Some devote their lives to proclaiming their children, others to proclaiming their football clubs, others to proclaiming their business, and others to proclaiming themselves. But Paul's life was utterly devoted to proclaiming "the gospel of God's grace".

Many Christians assume that "the gospel" is everything good about being Christian, but that's not what the Bible says! Since the gospel is "the power of God that brings salvation" (Romans 1:16), we need to know what the gospel really is so that we can be saved and then proclaim it to our families, friends and colleagues, so they can be saved too.

The word "gospel" just means "good news". It was used in the

Roman Empire of New Testament times for momentous public announcements such as the birth of an emperor or a victory in battle. The "gospel of God" is his sensational announcement to his world, progressively revealed in the Bible (Romans 1:1-17).

In the Old Testament, God's gospel promised a kingdom and a King

One of the earliest announcements of the gospel was in God's promise to Abraham of a land, a nation and blessing—a kingdom to bring blessing to all nations (Genesis 12:1-3). Israel's history then provides an earthly picture of the heavenly kingdom through which such global blessing will come.

God announced his "gospel" again in Isaiah's repeated promises of a King for his kingdom. The Lord himself would come to rule and liberate his people from their exile far from God, and gather them into his kingdom. Amazingly, this deliverer would be the Lord's suffering servant, dying under the penalty for our sin and then rising to life for our "justification" (God's acceptance) (Isaiah 40, 52, 61, 53).

God provided many judges, priests, kings and governors with different roles that point to his King, and sent many prophets to describe him in the most exalted terms. But then there was silence for centuries... until the explosive moment when a tradesman's "son" emerged onto the public stage, "proclaiming the good news (gospel) of God. 'The time has come,' he said. 'The kingdom of God has come near. Repent and believe the good news!'" (Mark 1:15)

In the New Testament, God's gospel announces that Jesus is our Lord and Saviour

The mystery of the gospel now becomes crystal clear in the New Testament as Jesus is unveiled as the long-awaited King, saving us into his kingdom. There are many versions of God's gospel, because it's about a person and not a formula. But two glorious themes emerge in them all: Jesus is our Lord (the theme of who he is) and Jesus is our Saviour (the theme of what he has done). Both are stunningly good news for us today.

Jesus is our Lord!

In Romans, Paul explains the gospel of God to show why all nations need to hear it. He says it's "regarding his Son". If we're not talking about Jesus, we're not talking about the gospel. When we talk about our experience, our church, our sin, or even God the Father and God the Holy Spirit, we are speaking of great biblical truths but not about the gospel that saves people.

So, the words of that famous Bible verse—"for God so loved the world" (John 3:16)—are not the gospel but the *reason* for the gospel. "That he gave his one and only Son" is the gospel. And "whoever believes in him shall not perish but have eternal life" is not the gospel but the *result* of the gospel. This is important to know so that we don't think that just proclaiming God's love, or just talking about believing, can save anyone; we need to speak about God's sacrificial gift of his Son if anyone is to be saved!

Paul often summarises God's gospel regarding his Son with the phrase, "Jesus Christ our Lord" (Romans 1:4; Colossians 2:6; 2 Corinthians 4:5, compare with Acts 2:36). Obviously, this isn't his first name, middle name and surname:

- *Jesus* means the crucified Galilean of history.
- *Christ* means the chosen Saviour King promised by Old Testament prophets.
- *Lord* means the divine and risen Ruler of all.

God's gospel tells us how amazing Jesus is: Jesus is Christ our Lord. It then tells us what he's done...

Jesus is our Saviour!

God's gospel celebrates Christ's four primary achievements:

1. **Christ came as our King** (Mark 1:14-15): Mark's Gospel is entitled, "The good news [gospel] about Jesus the Messiah, the Son of God [divine King]", and then announces, "Jesus went into Galilee, proclaiming the good news [gospel] of God ... The kingdom of God has come near!" Jesus is the long-awaited King, rescuing people and bringing them into his heavenly kingdom. He demonstrated the fabulous benefits of life under his rule with his merciful forgiveness, wise teaching and compassionate miracles. Although the Gospels climax in recounting Jesus' death and resurrection, Acts describes the Apostles preaching Christ's resurrection from the dead, and the epistles concentrate on the gospel of Christ and him crucified. This is not different to Jesus' gospel of the kingdom, for we enter his kingdom by being united by faith with his death and resurrection; the cross is how our King opened the way into his kingdom.

2. **Christ died for our sins** (1 Corinthians 15:1-4): Paul reminds the Corinthians of God's saving gospel: "Christ died for our sins according to the Scriptures". Christ's death was incredibly special because he died (voluntarily and not as a victim) for our sins (as our loving self-sacrificial substitute) according to the Scriptures (to satisfy the justice of God as our "Passover sacrifice", our "Atonement sacrifice" and our "Suffering Servant sacrifice"). Paul then reminds his readers that Christ's death is absolutely undeniable because he was buried!

3. **Christ rose to rule** (1 Corinthians 15:4-7): Paul continues, "He was raised on the third day according to the Scriptures". The New Testament triumphantly proclaims that, as

promised by the Old Testament and by Jesus himself, he was raised to life and enthroned in heaven as King over us all because he completely paid for all our sins—and so we are completely qualified for heaven in him. Paul reminds us that his resurrection is absolutely undeniable because "he appeared" to many people on multiple public occasions.

4. **Christ will return to judge** (Romans 2:16): Many Christians are unaware that Scripture explicitly says that judgment is part of the gospel, as in Romans 2:16: "the day when God judges people's secrets through Jesus Christ, as my gospel declares". Christ's judgment will begin the punishment of the unrepentant wicked in hell, as well as his extravagant blessing of his forgiven people in his beautiful new creation.

The spectacular benefits of God's gospel are life in his heavenly kingdom

God's gospel is also described in Scripture as the gospel of peace, hope, life and righteousness—and here as "the gospel of God's grace". These are the wonderful benefits of the gospel for all who believe it.

When we turn to Jesus, we begin to daily experience the reassuring comfort of peace with God even in the midst of tragedy and pain, the uplifting encouragement of our certain hope of being with him, the deep satisfaction of life in personal relationship with him, and the joy of Christ's righteousness both counted as ours and growing within us; that is, we've begun to enjoy the incredible generosity of God's grace. And one day, when Jesus returns, we'll know these joys perfectly in heaven. These blessings of the gospel are together actually life in the kingdom of God, the glorious blessing originally promised to Abraham.

Conclusion: The gospel is the joyful message of God's grace

The gospel declares joyful news: Jesus is Christ our Lord, who came as our King, died for our sins, rose to rule and will return to judge; in other words, Jesus is our Lord and Saviour. Mind you, I have discovered rather painfully that we can think we're proclaiming the gospel of grace when the way we do it drains all the goodness out of it. Some years ago, a Scottish minister friend confronted me: "There's not enough grace in your preaching," he said. "It's all challenge!" I was mortified. But he was right! Whenever I challenged the congregation, "You should realise how marvellous the grace of God is", my challenge was undermining the sheer wonder of the gospel. I needed to feel and find language that simply marvels at "the gospel of God's grace".

For there's nothing for us to be or to do for our salvation but to enjoy who Christ is and what he has done for us. The "gospel of God's grace" that Paul proclaimed is not good advice for us to follow, or good ideas for us to discuss, but good news for us to celebrate!

Think it through

1. *What is dangerous about thinking the gospel is about something other than Jesus Christ our Lord?*

2. *What aspects of the gospel do you find most exciting?*

3. *In what way is the gospel about God's grace? How are you tempted to undermine this?*

Church leaders: *How can you ensure that the gospel of the Bible outlined above is clearly believed and proclaimed in your church?*

10. Preach the kingdom

because the best is yet to come

*"Now I know that none of you among whom I have gone
about preaching the kingdom will ever see me again."*
Acts 20:25

The world was reeling in shock. Over 500,000 dead, millions homeless, 100,000 children orphaned, whole communities flattened. The pictures of devastation caused by the earthquake and tsunami of Boxing Day 2004 were heartbreaking. None more than the harrowing images of bewildered children, too traumatised to cry, gazing over desolate landscapes searching for their families.

Everywhere, people were not only horrified by the scale of this tragedy but confused by the spiritual implications. We recognise that Hitler, Stalin and Pol Pot were homicidal tyrants. We know that Stalingrad and Auschwitz were tragedies born of a wicked human ideology. We realise that the devastation of 9/11 and Syria involve complex politico-religious conflicts for which human beings are responsible. But this tsunami wasn't a genocide, war or terrorist attack with a tyrant, government or suicide bomber to blame. It was tragedy without purpose! How could God allow such dreadful suffering?

Just as horrifying are the incessant reports of brutal persecution of Christians in North Korea, Eritrea, Iraq, Afghanistan, Sudan and Iran, especially with the rise of Islamic extremist groups such as Boko Haram and ISIS (Daesh). While estimates of killings for Christian faith vary hugely (the causes are often complicated), perhaps the most reliable figure is that of the Open Doors watchdog, reckoning that 7,000 of our brothers and sisters were killed for their faith in Christ in the year to October 2015 (the highest year to date), while an estimated 70-80,000 Christians are currently held in North Korean labour camps.

Countless believers around the globe suffer beatings, threats, and economic and social prejudice. What's the problem? Is God unable to help his children or... unwilling?

For others of us, it isn't natural disasters or vindictive persecution that undermine our faith in God. It's a cancer that puts a loved one in a wheelchair or an early grave. And there's always the gnawing disappointment that our marriage, or career, or children, or churches—indeed our lives—aren't what we'd hoped they'd be. How can a living and loving God allow so much misery in his world?

Doesn't he care?

Of course, in the midst of anguish and suffering we don't need pious platitudes and theological debate. We need someone to be there for us, to cry with us and carry us. But for those at a greater distance from suffering, as we reflect upon it and prepare for it, everyone wonders why the God we worship doesn't stop the pain.

Alternatives

The dominant religions of the world don't offer much comfort. For example, in the regions struck by that Boxing Day tsunami, **Hinduism**, the dominant faith of India, regards suffering as being deserved for the evil we have done in previous incarnations. The balancing force of *karma* is just something inevitable that we must learn to accept.

Islam, the dominant religion of Indonesia, regards suffering as determined by the will of Allah—his "finger of judgment" upon human wickedness—to which we must submit.

Buddhism, the dominant religion of Sri Lanka, regards suffering as a kind of illusion caused by frustrated longings of love—which we must learn to ignore!

Faced with such uninspiring alternatives, many retreat to atheistic despair or scientific cynicism, where tragedy is just the unfortunate collision of powerful natural forces. Biologist Richard Dawkins propounds this idea with brutal clarity:

> *"In a universe of blind physical forces and genetic replication, some people are going to get hurt, other people are going to get lucky, and you won't find any rhyme or reason in it, nor any justice."*
> River Out of Eden: A Darwinian View of Life, p 131-132

But disbelieving in God doesn't make the world any better. It just makes life more pointless and hopeless! Many assume that suffering undermines Christian faith because they think we believe in a God who's desperately trying, but obviously failing, to be nice. They think natural disasters prove either that he's not loving (because he won't stop suffering) or that he's not powerful (because he can't stop suffering). They conveniently forget the alternative: that more good could come from a loving and powerful God allowing disasters and suffering while he unfolds his long-term plan for countless people to find comfort and blessings in a paradise kingdom yet to come!

Actually, the Bible is full of deep reflection upon human suffering, including whole books such as Job, Habakkuk, 1 Peter and the Gospels. For we follow a King who took flesh to endure homelessness, prejudice, betrayal, torture and crucifixion so that we can enter his heavenly kingdom.

But how can Christians trust in a living and loving God who allows suffering? The answer lies in understanding the kingdom of God—where it is and why it's delayed...

The unfolding history of God's kingdom

The whole Bible is essentially the history of God establishing his eternal kingdom. There are four stages to this drama. And each reveals something of the kingdom God will establish one day:

1. God's kingdom was revealed *(Genesis to Joshua)*

In the beginning, God created a kingdom on earth, in which he ruled our ancestors, Adam and Eve, in a paradise garden, blessing them with his presence and law. But they rebelled and were expelled, condemned to die.

However, God promised to renew his kingdom for all nations through a descendant of Abraham. God preserved Abraham's family despite sin, infertility and famine, and raised up Jacob's despised son, Joseph, to become prime minister to save the family (much as Jesus would be despised by men but exalted by God to save his church family). When the people were enslaved in Egypt, the LORD redeemed them through Moses, by power over Pharaoh and a Passover sacrifice; he brought Israel across the Red Sea to himself at Mount Sinai and gave them his law so they would know how to worship him; he provided them with a sacrificial system for pardon and cleansing, and led them through the desert to the promised land; despite the rebellions of the people, the LORD led them victoriously into their inheritance in the promised land of Canaan through Joshua ("Jesus"). This first portion of Scripture is generally employed by the New Testament writers to explain how we are redeemed from captivity to Satan, sin and death by God's power and Passover sacrifice on the cross, and brought into his promised kingdom of heaven.

2. God's kingdom was ruled *(Judges to Song of Songs)*

We're then introduced to life in God's earthly kingdom under judges, prophets, priests, kings and governors. These spirit-filled but imperfect leaders combine to give us a profile of the promised Messiah (or "Christ", meaning "chosen" and "anointed") to save us.

Saul was the first messiah-king: chosen by God, anointed by God's prophet, filled with God's Spirit and victorious for God's people. But he disobeyed God. So God then chose David, the warrior king, likewise anointed, Spirit-filled and victorious over the giant enemy of Israel, Goliath. David was then promised a son who would rule for ever, but he rebelled in murderous adultery with Bathsheba.

David's son, Solomon, the prince of peace, was brilliantly wise; he established peace with surrounding nations and built a great temple for God to which people could come with prayers and sacrifices for forgiveness. The kingdom of Israel was at its most glorious under Solomon, and the Queen of Sheba was blown away: "How happy your people must be! How happy your officials, who continually stand before you and hear your wisdom!" (1 Kings 10:8). This prosperous, safe and happy kingdom gives a glimpse of the happiness to come from being governed by the chosen King to come, Jesus.

Tragically, Solomon's heart was led astray by his many wives and concubines to worship foreign idols. In judgment, Israel was plunged into civil war under a succession of dreadfully wicked kings. In 722 BC, the northern kingdom of Israel was conquered by Assyria. In 596-586 BC, the southern kingdom of Judah was conquered by Babylon and its people were taken into exile. The exiles included fine young leaders like Daniel, taken to be indoctrinated in pagan life in Babylon University. But Daniel resolved not to defile himself (Daniel 1:8) in the pagan city, because "the Most High is sovereign over all kingdoms on earth" (Daniel 4:32)—or, as the New Testament puts it, "Jesus is Lord" (Romans 10:9). The exiles now waited for the LORD to come to redeem them in order to bring them home to his kingdom. This portion of Scripture is used often in the New Testament to describe the promised King.

3. God's kingdom was promised *(Isaiah to Malachi)*
Throughout the history of Israel, God's prophets warned the kings, and then the people, of God's coming wrath upon their idolatry. But they also promised God's abundant blessings in his resurrected kingdom. Using the language of earthly Israel, the prophets promised a glorious new kingdom with a renewed creation, city and temple for a resurrected international people, redeemed by a divine King who would be both a transcendent "son of man" and a humble "suffering servant". This part of Scripture is used in the New Testament to paint pictures of life in the kingdom of heaven.

4. God's kingdom is coming *(Matthew to Revelation)*
When God's King finally arrived, he was not what people were expecting. He was a meek and compassionate servant of sinners. But his miraculous power over disaster, disease, demons and death revealed both his divine identity and the

future blessings of the kingdom he will bring one day. Christ came as our representative King, he died for our sins, he rose to rule, and he will one day return to judge his enemies, reward his servants and renew his creation. He opened the way for sinners into his kingdom by dying on a cross to endure the punishment we deserve for our sin and to complete the righteous Christian life we need to qualify us for heaven.

The risen Christ appointed his apostolic witnesses to clarify in their New Testament writings that by faith-union with Christ we become citizens of his heavenly kingdom, but his kingdom is "not of this world" (John 18:36). When we obey Jesus' command to pray "your kingdom come" (Matthew 6:10), we ask God to extend the rule of his kingdom into the hearts of people around the world through the gospel, and plead with him to come soon because it hurts down here. God sustains us with his "common grace" in this world, but his kingdom is not, as some suggest, to be found wherever there is justice. God's kingdom is wherever Christ reigns, in the hearts of believers who accept the gospel message that he is King and surrender to his rule. His kingdom grows as Christ calls more sinners through the gospel to surrender to his rule and become citizens of his coming heavenly kingdom.

This all means that Christians on earth aren't yet immune to the sin of our fallen nature, or the corruption of our decaying bodies, or the pain of a world under God's judgment. For the history of the kingdom of God in the Bible isn't just useful historical background. Rather, it is vital to understand the chronology of God's kingdom to cope with the pain and disappointments of life. So much of our discontent stems from inflated expectations of life in this world resulting from failing to understand the delay in the coming of God's kingdom. There are two vital implications:

The King allows suffering until his kingdom comes

God governs every detail of our universe, including disasters and pain. But God isn't the source of evil and he takes no joy in the foretaste of judgment that he sends upon the world when stirring up earthquakes and tsunamis. "I take no pleasure in the death of the wicked, but rather that they turn from their ways and live" (Ezekiel 33:11). God is working out his sovereign plans to save countless people from all nations and cultures. The Boxing Day tsunami should cause us to fear, not just the oceans, but the God who moves them. Indeed, C.S. Lewis wrote, "God whispers to us in our pleasures, speaks in our consciences, but shouts in our pains. It is his megaphone to rouse a deaf world" (*The Problem of Pain*). And Christians learn in the midst of suffering how to trust our Father while we wait to be rescued. I know that when my wife and I have been through periods fearing the loss of a child, we have found, as others have, that our Father did not answer our prayers to quickly remove us from our pain; rather, he quickly sent his people into our pain to carry us when we were too weak to stand, and taught us to depend upon others while we were forced to wait for his relief.

The King came to save us from suffering and brings us into his kingdom

We're tempted to yell at God, "Why don't you do something?" Since 30,000 children die daily from poverty caused by unequal distribution of food, God could reasonably ask, "Why don't *you* do something?"

But instead, God has done something quite sensational about the suffering in the world.

Despite our rebellious disobedience, God still loves us passionately. He shrank himself down into an ordinary man from Galilee, to swap places with ordinary people like us in suffering our hell on the cross. There he drained into his soul every last drop of the acid cup of God's wrath, so that none remains for us; and he completed a perfect Christian life of obedience that qualifies us for heaven. The Bible describes his pain-free paradise in beautifully personal terms:

> "God himself will be with them and be their God. 'He will wipe every tear from their eyes. There will be no more death' or mourning or crying or pain, for the old order of things has passed away."   Revelation 21:3-4

No more mass graves, grief-stricken parents or bewildered orphans. No more persecution or disappointments. The gospel of the kingdom of God is marvellous news of spectacular hope for a grief-stricken world writhing in pain. God has acted to rescue us from hell for heaven for ever, in the costly sacrifice of his only beloved Son on the cross. To *allow* a saving sacrifice is grace; to *provide* this saving sacrifice is amazing grace; to *become* this saving sacrifice is grace beyond our wildest dreams. Like Paul, Reformed churches like ours will proclaim the kingdom of heaven—not just as a history lesson, but as an assurance of hope in the midst of hardship and pain: the chronology of the kingdom of God tells us, "The best is yet to come".

Or, as the Bachman-Turner Overdrive classic reminds us, "Baby, you just ain't seen nothin' yet!"

Think it through

1. *What is more comforting to you in the midst of suffering— knowing that Jesus has also suffered, or knowing that his coming kingdom will be free of all pain and suffering?*

2. *How would you answer someone who said that they could not believe in a God of love because of all the suffering in the world?*

3. *Suffering will come to us all, so it would be wise to spend some time praying now. Pray that the Spirit would drive these truths deep into your heart—so that you flee to God rather than flee from him when dark days come.*

Church leaders: *How could you give your church access to an understanding of the chronology of the kingdom of God in Scripture to help them cope with suffering?*

11. Warn about judgment

because we want to be innocent of blood

"Therefore, I declare to you today that I am innocent of the blood of any of you." Acts 20:26

During a week of outreach events that our church held to help our members witness to their friends and neighbours, we organised a "Lumberjack and Beer Night" for men. We invited a team of huge lumberjacks to come and smash up massive logs in the middle of our church, with 180 men gathered around cheering in the dark, like on the TV show "Top Gear". It proved very effective for getting local unbelievers in to hear a gospel message.

It was a fantastic atmosphere and a non-Christian friend of mine came with me. As senior pastor I was meant to follow the wood-chopping with a talk, but what should I speak about? John the Baptist warned about judgment, saying, "The axe has been laid to the root of the trees, and every tree that does not produce good fruit will be cut down and thrown into the fire" (Matthew 3:10). It was an obvious text. But I was worried I might scare the men away. And, to be honest, I was worried that they wouldn't like me very much. When I shared my anxiety with my wife, she said with gentle sarcasm, "Well, you could always tell them some popular lies that they want to hear, I suppose?"

I do love my wife.

Too often, we've thought that if we're nice enough for long enough people will eventually come to church to hear about Jesus and get saved. But more commonly, they just say, "Thanks for a great night—I'll come again next year!" I realised I had to give the men a better reason to come back and hear about Jesus than thinking I was a nice bloke, even if some of them wouldn't like me anymore. So I did speak about judgment and the cross, and a few guys didn't like it and left in disgust. But most of them stayed around for over an hour afterwards chatting—and the Christian guys were thrilled that I'd explained the hard truth of judgment, so they could talk about the Saviour.

It was a fantastic night—and I learned the lesson that my job is not just to be likeable, but to urge people to flee from God's wrath to God's Saviour. Instead of trying to be popular with all the guests, I needed to support our church men with their evangelism by saying some of the hard things they would find difficult to raise; that is, to set them up to talk more about the love of God in Christ. Indeed, if we won't talk about judgement, then we cannot say, as Paul says in this verse, "I am innocent of the blood of any of you". Let me explain.

He's using a frightening Old Testament image here. God is so reluctant to punish people that he appointed his prophet Ezekiel as a "watchman" to warn people to prepare for his judgment—like a watchman standing on the walls of an ancient town to warn townsfolk of approaching raiders. If they refused to listen, God wouldn't blame Ezekiel. But if he failed to warn them then, God said, "that wicked person will die for their sin, and I will hold you accountable for their blood" (Ezekiel 33:8).

Now, all Christians are God's prophets, required to proclaim the gospel message including "the day when God judges people's secrets through Jesus Christ, as my gospel declares" (Romans 2:16). Since Paul had faithfully warned the Ephesians about God's coming wrath, he was "innocent of [their] blood". However, it remains a truly dreadful prospect that we could arrive in heaven spattered with the blood of the bewildered unbelievers we failed to warn!

When we pray for spiritual revival like that of the "evangelical revivals" in England and America in the 1730s, it's sobering to recognise that God used preachers such as Wesley, Whitfield and Edwards to boldly proclaim both the glory of Christ and the horrors of hell in the most terrifying terms. The great Aberavon-Revival preacher Martyn Lloyd-Jones once declared, "I'm not afraid of being charged, as I frequently am, with trying to frighten you, for I am definitely trying to do so. If the wondrous love of God in Christ Jesus and the hope of glory is not sufficient to attract you, then, such is the value I attach to the worth of your soul, I will do my utmost to alarm you with a sight of the terrors of hell."

It's the wrath of God that reveals our need of a Saviour to suffer our hell on the cross. And though the benefits of being a Christian are not always obvious now, the eternal gulf between believers at home with God in heaven and unbelievers in everlasting conscious torment in hell could not be more extreme. If we, our churches or our evangelistic courses fail to warn people of judgment, heaven and hell, we're not "innocent of the blood of any of you". We'll explore the joy of heaven when we consider Acts 20 verse 32. Here, we must face four facts that Paul explains elsewhere about God's day of judgment, when Christ returns:

> "God is just: he will pay back trouble to those who trouble you and give relief to you who are troubled, and to us as well. This will happen when the Lord Jesus is revealed from heaven in blazing fire with his powerful angels. He will punish those who do not know God and do not obey the gospel of our Lord Jesus. They will be punished with everlasting destruction and shut out from the presence of the Lord." 2 Thessalonians 1:6-9

The judgment will be fair *"God is just" (v 6)*

God is absolutely fair and entirely free of any unjust leniency or cruelty. No one can bribe, threaten or confuse him. He knows all the facts with perfect recall. He will judge our thoughts, words and deeds impartially, and his punishments will perfectly fit people's crimes (Matthew 12:36; Revelation 20:12; 1 Peter 1:17; Romans 2:6). God will take into account all mitigating circumstances such as lesser knowledge or difficult circumstances as well as condemning privileges and opportunities for faith.

By God's amazing grace, those who trust in Jesus will have his perfect Christian life of good works credited to us so that we are justly acceptable in his righteousness. Incredibly, God even wants to fairly reward us for the good works that his Spirit has empowered in us.

The judge will be Jesus *"When the Lord Jesus is revealed" (v 7)*

Jesus will appear personally in fiery holiness with powerful angels. The Old Testament promised God's arrival as a "refiner's fire" on a day that will "burn like a furnace" (Malachi 3:1-2; 4:1). Jesus is that God—engulfing unrepentant sinners in his holy wrath like a raging bushfire engulfing dry grass.

Jesus lovingly warns us, "The angels will come and separate the wicked from the righteous and throw them into the blazing furnace, where there will be weeping and gnashing of teeth" (Matthew 13:49-50). This horrible image of living for ever in the excruciating agony of a furnace is accurate because "our God is a consuming fire" (Hebrews 12:29). Arriving in the presence of God unprotected by the righteous life of Christ is rather like arriving on the surface of the sun naked. Paul is not describing a despicable medieval instrument of torture that God deploys, but an eternity for unpardoned sinners in the presence of a holy God. God will not light a fire. His holiness is the fire in the furnace.

And Jesus won't come alone. His vast army of angels expresses both his personal majesty and his power to gather the living and the dead from all corners of the earth; he will be like a farmer, swinging a sickle to harvest grapes for crushing in the winepress of his wrath until an ocean of blood flows out in all directions (Daniel 7; Revelation 14). No one will escape.

The charge will be neglect *"He will punish those who do not know God and do not obey the gospel of our Lord Jesus" (v 8)*

Most people think that God will weigh our good deeds against our bad deeds, and only a few tyrants and mass-murderers will go to hell. But the two-part description of our primary human crime here is not one of wicked activity but wicked inactivity: a neglect of God and his gospel.

God will not punish anyone for rejecting Christ if they've never heard of Christ (like ancient Aborigines, isolated Amazonian jungle-dwellers, or those trapped in religious fanaticism). But God *will* punish them for rejecting God, of whom they are well aware from the grandeur of creation; for we constantly redesign God with our imagination into our preferred or inherited religious images.

Many are guilty of further neglect, if we "do not obey the gospel" when we hear it. There will be more terrible consequences for the people of Capernaum and London who have heard and rejected the gospel than for pagans from cities like Tyre and Riyadh who have never heard the gospel in language they can understand. Many will protest that they don't *hate* God. But they have *neglected* his crucified Son. Which is heartbreaking because...

The punishment will be dreadful *"They will be punished with everlasting destruction and shut out from the presence of the Lord" (v 9)*

Jesus warned of the horrors of hell with many descriptions. Paul selects two. "Everlasting destruction" doesn't mean annihilation but ruin. Everything good and dignified from God in us will be stripped away to reveal all that is foul within us—hating and being hated in hell. Jesus said sinners will suffer in the shrivelled isolation of despair, racked with sobbing and pain. Worst of all, it will never, ever end, for hell must be as permanent as heaven (Matthew 25:46).

We may complain that eternity in hell seems too harsh for one short lifetime of sin. But the magnitude of a crime is increased by the status of the person against whom it is committed. And awful sins that are committed in just a moment of hatred remain permanent to God. Hell is God's holy place, and he is as eternally present in hell to punish as he is present in heaven to bless. Sadly, there's no indication that unbelievers in hell ever want to turn to God.

If we won't talk to people about the punishment we all deserve for our sin, the death of Christ in our place on the cross will never seem very necessary or wonderful. The best way to do this in Western cultures is usually to speak of what we now realise we ourselves deserve, rather than accusing people directly.

We find it hard to imagine how we'll ever be able to accept God's punishment of our loved ones in hell. I don't know, but maybe—as we already want a sadistic paedophile to be justly punished—when we finally recognise the true horror of our own sin, we'll marvel not at the sufferings of hell but at the blessings of heaven, stunned more by God's grace than his judgment.

Reformed churches like our Co-Mission churches are urgent about evangelism because we know that the gospel announces God's judgment. To be "innocent of ... blood" and to love the lost, without using cruel medieval imagery or being eager to condemn or remotely self-righteous, we must find loving and appropriate ways to warn people to flee from the wrath to come... to Jesus.

Think it through

1. *Do you believe that you deserve God's judgment?*

2. *Do you talk about the judgment of God when you share the gospel? If not, why not?*

3. *Have you ever prayed something like this to become a Christian, and be saved from the wrath to come?*
   "Dear Lord Jesus, SORRY for my sin. THANK YOU for dying for me. PLEASE forgive me and help me turn from sin to follow you."
   If not, pray this now to be saved!

Church leaders: *How can you ensure that judgment, heaven and hell are given appropriate emphasis in the teaching and evangelism of your church?*

12. Tell the whole truth

because a distorted gospel doesn't save

"For I have not hesitated to proclaim to you the whole will of God." Acts 20:27

A close friend of mine is a professional musician. He tours the world as the drummer for a rock band playing packed venues and some of the biggest shows in London. I long for him to become a Christian, so when he's home we often discuss the Bible. But he and his wife really struggle with the Bible's teaching on sexual morality. Sometimes I wish I could just rip out the politically incorrect pages of Scripture. Then he might get saved... and play in our church band. That would be awesome!

But Paul didn't pull back from teaching "the whole will of God" in the Bible, however unpopular it was. He later instructed Timothy, "Preach the word; be prepared in season and out of season" (2 Timothy 4:2). This means teaching God's Word faithfully, whether or not it's comfortable for the audience (challenging their views or lifestyle) and whether or not it's comfortable for the teacher (who finds it difficult to disappoint people).

We must teach the Bible "in season", when it's fruitful and the church grows, but also "out of season", when it isn't welcome and the church shrinks. Paul says the reason the Word will not always be welcome is because "people will not put up with sound [healthy] doctrine" (2 Timothy 4:3). For even if the Bible is not always what people want, it is nevertheless always what they need—for spiritual health. Many will prefer the ridiculous myths of TV prosperity preachers promising wealth, or the lies of liberal preachers permitting immorality. But faithful teachers must proclaim the truth, the whole truth and nothing but the truth.

This includes unpopular doctrines such as the uniqueness of Christ, the eternity of hell, the evil of hedonism, the headship of men and the need for sexual purity. This is certainly no charter for cruel insensitivity; rather, Bible-centred churches such as ours are committed to lovingly teaching all of God's will in Scripture—and supporting others in doing the same.

Clashes between God's Word and modern culture are often helped by understanding God

Genesis reveals that God designed mankind to be like him for a relationship with him. This has a profound effect upon how human relationships flourish today. In Western cultures, it's often helpful to appreciate the nature of God before trying to commend or defend his rules for our social behaviour.

Jesus endorsed the teaching of Scripture that there's only one God who is a unity of three Persons: Father, Son and Holy Spirit. This holy Trinity lives in a permanent, plural, equal, complementary, ordered, loving union. Since we're created like him, it's important to realise that we thrive in relationships like his:

- **God is permanent:** So humans usually flourish in lasting rather than transitory relationships. That's why it's generally better for children to be raised in a stable family than to be repeatedly moved around foster homes; and it's why God wants lasting marriages rather than serial co-habitations.

- **God is plural:** So humans usually flourish better in community than in isolation. That's why it's generally beneficial to live in some kind of family, and to have close friends and take part in a local community, and to work in teams rather than living in lonely isolation (even when surrounded by virtual crowds on screens); and it's why, as God saves us, he places us into our churches to enjoy all of these benefits.

- **God is equal:** So human beings of every age, race, economic status and sexuality are equally precious to God. That's why God wants us to invest sacrificially in social welfare and endeavour to ensure that the poor, disabled and disadvantaged are cared for as well as the wealthy, strong and privileged; and it's why men and women should respect each other as having equal dignity and value before God.

- **God is complementary:** So human beings generally flourish better in diverse social contexts than in monochrome environments. That's why God has designed us to flourish in multi-cultural societies; and this complementary diversity is why God's version of marriage is heterosexual.

- **God is ordered:** So human relationships flourish where there is both loving authority and humble submission that never imply any superiority or inferiority. As Christ leads the church but submits to his Father, someone can exercise authority over her children and her staff team but submit to the authority of her employer, church Elder and husband, and be absolutely equal in importance and dignity with them all; after all, we expect employees to submit to their employers and children to submit to their parents and citizens to submit to police officers without ever thinking them inferior! And it's why husbands can lovingly lead their wives and their wives lovingly submit to their husbands, in serving God together without ever implying inequality.

- **God is loving:** So the most precious aspect of all our human relationships is to love and be loved. Real love is not merely sentimental affection or sensual desire but sacrificial kindness, based not upon another's performance but upon a promise, a covenant to serve the interests of another; and this is why married Christians will keep working at their marriage through difficult seasons rather than contemplate divorce.

Having understood how the nature of God impacts human relationships in general, we're better placed to understand marriage and sexual morality. Contrary to much contemporary thinking, our fundamental identity and value lie in being created in the image of God rather than in our sexuality. This is why Christians celebrate the dignity of childhood and celibate singleness, and don't idolise marriage or sexual activity as essential to wellbeing. Jesus made it very clear that...

God designed marriage as the lifelong union of one man and one woman

Jesus explained:

> "At the beginning the Creator 'made them male and female', and said, 'For this reason a man will leave his father and mother and be united to his wife, and the two will become one flesh.'" Matthew 19:4-5

Jesus taught that God created us in his likeness to be diverse in gender, namely male or female. Most of us feel comfortable with this.

But we have become very conscious in Western culture today of those who are "transgender" (an umbrella description of people who experience the feeling that their gender is not the same as, or does not sit comfortably with, their biological sex). Their struggles have been highlighted by the public transitioning of former decathlon world-record holder Caitlin Jenner, by the film "The Danish Girl" about the artist Lili Elbe, who was one of the first to undergo sex-change surgery, and by increasingly wide-ranging debates about which restrooms people who identify as transgender should use, which prison a transgender criminal should be sent to, and what passport identity is appropriate for those in this situation.

These are complex conditions experienced by precious people, all created in the image of the God who loves them deeply, and who often suffer the distress and loneliness of "gender dysphoria" (feelings of discomfort because of a mismatch between their biological sex and their internal sense of gender identity). A very small number of people are "intersex" (born with biological attributes that make it unclear which sex they are, and where it may continue to be unclear until they are older).

Secular Western culture urges us to assert our individual *autonomy*, including a right to determine our own sexual identity; it prizes personal *authenticity*, that I am whoever I feel myself to be and should resist anyone imposing their view of my identity upon me. However, Jesus is teaching in this passage that we are all created and loved by God and embodied to be sexual. As the pastor and author Vaughan Roberts puts it:

> *"The basic message of creation is this: each person's biologically-determined sex is a good gift of God's creation. We should accept it and live within it."* Transgender, p 43

As one Christian writer—who struggles with same-sex attraction but remains committed to biblical celibacy—tweeted:

> *"Our culture says: your psychology is your sexual identity— let your body be conformed to it; the Bible says: your body is your sexual identity—let your mind be conformed to it."*

So our gender, even where it feels confused within us, is a biological gift from God and not merely a lifestyle choice or the product of our upbringing. Indeed, our bi-gender diversity is a beautiful reflection of diversity within the persons of God in the Trinity.

This, says Jesus, is why God's version of marriage is the permanent union of a man and woman, expressed in the intimate pleasure of sex, as the ideal social environment for creating and raising children. Paul explains elsewhere that such marriage is a powerful illustration of Christ's sacrificial love for his church (Ephesians 5:22-33). We could invent any number of alternative kinds of stable relationship, and many Western nations have legalised same-sex marriage, but it isn't what Jesus means by marriage unless it is the publicly recognised union of a man and a woman.

Moreover, it's true that Jesus nowhere explicitly condemns homosexual desire or activity (though many other parts of the Bible explicitly do, such as Romans 1 and 1 Corinthians 6). Indeed, there are many kinds of sexual behaviour that Jesus doesn't explicitly condemn. Instead, Jesus clarifies what marriage is so that we will understand that other kinds of sexual relationship are not marriage nor permissible.

The relief of the gospel is that although we have all been sexually corrupt in different ways, we are all welcome to come to Jesus for his total forgiveness and transforming power to learn how we can be holy for him. It is probably helpful when defending the wisdom of God's condemnation of homosexual activity to emphasise that all sexual activity outside marriage, whether heterosexual or homosexual, is forbidden by God's Word (and called *porneia* in the original Greek, from which we get our word pornography). Christians are not homophobic, but pornophobic! And believers who want to follow Jesus but have desires that are not permitted in Scripture, whether heterosexual or homosexual (and whether legalised or not), will bravely commit themselves to be celibate and enjoy the strengthening of God's Spirit and the warm encouragements of their church in doing so.

Most Christians find themselves having to suppress powerful sexual desires of different kinds. Reformed churches like ours are committed to teaching and living by the whole counsel of God, even when it's politically incorrect to do so, because we trust that our Creator understands us and wants the very best for our relationships. These issues of marriage, sexual ethics and gender identity are causing increasing tension between Christians and secular authorities, especially now that many of them are being dealt with under "equality" legislation.

In every generation, Christian churches have had to contend for the faith of the Bible within their own congregations, with other church leaders that compromise with the prevailing culture, and with state authorities suppressing Christian faith. Christians in many Western nations have enjoyed for many centuries a freedom to openly practise their faith without censure that persecuted believers in other continents can only dream of. This freedom is gradually disappearing. The Apostle Paul faced aggressive persecution from Jewish religious leaders and Roman state authorities everywhere he went. Yet we read his statement, "I have not hesitated to proclaim to you the whole will of God". Let us take courage to follow his example, as he followed the example of our Lord, who was nailed to a cross by the religious and state authorities of his day. Teach "the whole will of God", even if those you long to see converted will never play in your church band, because you are teaching... the will of God!

Think it through

1. *What part of the Bible's teaching do you find most awkward when sharing the gospel with unbelievers?*

2. *Is it surprising that the Bible would differ from our culture in the areas of marriage, sexual ethics and gender identity?*

3. *How does tying marriage and sex to the character of God help your understanding of this issue?*

Church leaders: *How can you ensure that your church members of all ages are appropriately hearing clear and faithful Bible-teaching about sexual morality?*

13. Pastor the flock

the way the Good Shepherd does it

"Keep watch over yourselves and all the flock of which the Holy Spirit has made you overseers. Be shepherds of the church." Acts 20:28

There's often confusion in churches about what is meant by "pastoral ministry". Many people think it's primarily about personal care and therapeutic counselling. So a clergyman may be described as a good Bible-teacher but a poor pastor—meaning he lacks the emotional intelligence to listen well or to help those who are struggling. And if church members think that pastoral ministry is about hospital visiting, marriage counselling and conflict resolution, they will be increasingly discontented if their "pastor" neglects these things!

But Paul teaches that the whole congregation is expected to "carry each other's burdens" (Galatians 6:2). Caring for each other is the responsibility of every Christian and not just church leaders (though church leaders will want to set a good example where they can).

So what was Paul telling the Ephesian Elders to do when he said, "Be shepherds", or "be pastors", of the church? Let's consider *what* pastoral ministry is, *who* should do it, and then *how* it should be done.

What is "pastoral ministry"?

When the Bible praises God as the "Shepherd" of Israel, he's praised for saving Israel from Egypt and leading them into the promised land—which is parallel with saving us and leading us into his heavenly kingdom. "He brought his people out like a flock; he led them like sheep through the wilderness" (Psalm 78:52). This is about more than kindness. It's about salvation.

Likewise, when the former shepherd King David famously wrote, "The LORD is my shepherd; I shall not want" (Psalm 23:1, ESV), he praised God for leading him through the valley of the shadow of death to feast in the house of the LORD for ever—meaning heaven. Again, this is about more than kindness—it's about salvation. God's "pastoral ministry" is not just personal care, but *saving* care—saving people and bringing them into his kingdom!

So, when we read of the LORD condemning the leaders of Israel (prophets, priests and kings) for not pastoring his sheep, it's clear from the context that the selfishness of these shepherds was not just a lack of personal kindness. They'd neglected to care enough for God's people to teach them from God's Word how to be saved, which resulted in the idolatry and immorality that was judged with exile to Babylon. In Ezekiel 34, we read of God rejecting these selfish pastors and promising to come and pastor his sheep himself. Here he beautifully describes what his "pastoral ministry" will involve. There are three themes with direct spiritual parallels in the ministry of Jesus and Paul, and which are required of all who pastor churches today:

1. **"Search ... rescue ... gather": the ministry of evangelism** (Ezekiel 34:11-13)

God first describes a ministry of *searching* for lost sheep, *rescuing* them from danger and *gathering* them to himself. We find this in the evangelistic ministry of Jesus. Indeed, he illustrates it with his tender parable about searching for a lost sheep and bringing it home with great joy (Luke 15:3-7). Paul followed Jesus' example in his unrelenting evangelism, cross-cultural mission and church-planting. He was *searching* for the lost who had been chosen by God for salvation, *rescuing* people from slavery to sin under God's judgment, and *gathering* them into God's church family. Pastoral ministry then and now begins with the searching, rescuing and gathering work of evangelism.

2. **"Pasture ... make them lie down ... bind up": the ministry of teaching** (Ezekiel 34:13-16)

Next, God says he will care for his flock by finding good *pasture* to feed his flock, locating safe places to *make them lie down* and rest, and *binding up* (healing) the wounds of injured sheep. God was promising that his pastoral ministry would include the spiritual equivalents of *feeding, resting* and *healing* people. Jesus did this through his various teaching ministries of public debates, synagogue sermons, small-group discussions and one-to-one biblical counselling. He provided good pasture to *feed* his sheep with when he saw with compassion the crowds as "like sheep without a shepherd ... [so] he began *teaching* them" (Mark 6:34). For God's Word is nourishment for our souls.

And he located the ideal place for spiritual rest when he said, "Come to me, all you who are weary and burdened, and ... you will find rest for your souls" (Matthew 11:28-29). For God's Word of grace relieves us from heavy burdens of guilt and fear.

And Jesus *healed* people spiritually (as well as physically) with his wise teaching. For the sound doctrine of God's Word gradually heals the damage of sin in our character and relationships.

We shall only be completely satisfied, rested and healthy in heaven, but good Bible-teaching helps us make progress. So Paul followed Jesus' example in his own teaching ministries and here encourages the Ephesian Elders to do the same. Then and now we gradually *feed, rest and heal* God's flock when we teach the Word of God. Saving pastoral ministry involves Biblical evangelism and teaching.

3. *"Justice ... judge ... save":* **the ministry of oversight** (Ezekiel 34:16-24):

Third, a shepherd in ancient times would need to govern his flock well. In Ezekiel, God speaks of judging between the sheep and strengthening the weak against the strong, who tread down their pasture, muddy their water and push them aside—to ensure that all the flock have access to food. This illustrates the spiritual necessity of protecting the quieter, weaker members of a local church from the noisy demands of the strong, to ensure that everyone is fairly provided for; for instance, the needs of the elderly or single mums or the disabled could be shamefully neglected in pandering to the demands of wealthy parents. Jesus was conspicuously forthright in confronting the powerful elites of his day, welcoming children, the disabled and social outcasts. Likewise, Paul reminds us of his concern to "help the weak" (Acts 20:35). So then and now, pastoral ministry includes wise judgment and compassionate protection to ensure that all God's people are cared for, especially in providing access to appropriate Word ministry.

So God's *pastoral ministry* involves Biblical *evangelism, teaching* and *oversight* of the flock—for their salvation.

Ezekiel promises that God would one day pastor God's people through King David. So Jesus, the Son of David, revealed himself to be this divine "Good Shepherd" who would lay down his life on the cross for his sheep (John 10). The Ephesian Elders, and all who are now appointed as pastors to shepherd his flock, must likewise give themselves sacrificially for Christ's sheep in evangelism (search-rescue-gathering), teaching (feed-rest-healing) and governing (fairly judging, protecting and allocating resources).

Most fundamentally, pastoral ministry begins with bringing people to the "Good Shepherd", who is the pastor people need: to Jesus. *But who is supposed to provide this pastoral ministry?*

Who are the Elders, Pastors and Overseers?

Notice some important terminology here. Paul was training "Elders" (the original word is "presbyters"), a term from village and synagogue life meaning a team of senior men (misleadingly translated "priest" in Roman Catholic and high Anglican circles).

But he also says that God has made them "overseers" (the original word is *episkopous*, often translated "bishops"); so in Scripture, the Elders of a local church are its bishops! Church leaders appointed to regional responsibilities (and sometimes today confusingly also called "bishops"), such as Titus, appointed to commission leaders for the churches of Crete (Titus 1), can be of great assistance to local churches, as in recent decades in Nigeria, where "missionary bishops" have led the churches in bold evangelism resulting in dramatic numbers of people turning to Christ amid violent persecution. But calling such regional leaders "bishops" can be unhelpful if it removes the vital responsibility for governance from the local church leadership or invites obstructive interference from regional leaders who are remote from the local church context. It is clear in this passage that local church *Elders* are the *overseers* with responsibility to *pastor* the church; that is, there is one combined leadership role of Elder-pastor-overseer. (Other passages reveal that the early churches also appointed "deacons" meaning "servants" or "ministers" for practical duties.)

Each of these three overlapping roles has a different emphasis. Some suggest that they derive from Christ's triple office as *Priest, Prophet* and *King* respectively. Amazingly, Scripture does proclaim the participation of all believers in these roles as part of our privilege of being in Christ—but doesn't ascribe any of these titles to leaders. Leaders today would therefore be wise to learn from Christ how to be exemplary Christians, but reserve these exalted titles for Christ alone.

Being an "Elder" brings authority to lead with wise decisions; being a "Pastor" brings responsibility to provide biblical evangelism, teaching and governance; being an "Overseer" brings responsibility to govern the church well; for example, to clarify, staff and finance the vision of the church, to appoint and equip leaders to recruit, train and manage ministry teams, and to develop appropriate strategies for making disciples of all nations for Christ. Leaders from different churches and constituencies will inevitably be stronger or weaker in different aspects of their pastoral ministry. Being sufficiently humble and self-reflective to recognise our weaknesses and seek help by building complementary teams is vital in a Christ-like Elder-pastor-overseer.

How are Elder-pastor-overseers to behave?

The Apostle Peter appealed to his fellow-Elders to "be shepherds of God's flock that is under your care", according to four behavioural principles (1 Peter 5:1-4)—like the four boundaries of a sports field within which to conduct their ministry.

- **"Watching over them"**—Elders must accept their collective responsibility for the welfare of the church; so however responsibilities are divided up between them—for example, in "purposeful" ministries or sub-committees—the Elders should avoid compartmentalising the church and washing their hands of those who are not their direct concern. They have a collective oversight.

- **"Not because you must, but because you are willing"**—Elders must serve with a cheerful sense of privilege rather than reluctant self-pity, however busy and stressed they may feel; any who don't want to serve as Elders should surely resign or take a break rather than complain and so dishonour the privilege of leading Christ's people.

- **"Not pursuing dishonest gain, but eager to serve"**—Elders must be careful to be givers rather than getters, contributing to churches rather than draining them. In particular, employed staff, who are entitled to respect and wages (1 Timothy 5:17-18), should repent of discontent or greed for a more comfortable lifestyle than is modest for their church. The people of Israel could commend the prophet Samuel: "You have not cheated or oppressed us" (1 Samuel 12:4). The Governor Nehemiah could say he "never demanded the food allotted to the governor, because the demands were heavy on the people" (Nehemiah 5:14-15). And the Apostle Paul was about to say, "These hands of mine have supplied my own needs and the needs of my companions" (Acts 20:34). Elder-pastor-overseers must serve like the one who said, "It is more blessed to give than to receive" (v 35).

- "Not lording it over those entrusted to you, but being examples to the flock"—Elders must not use their positions of authority to dominate or exalt themselves but humbly set a good example of what they teach. Whether we serve in a Western celebrity culture, African chieftain culture or Eastern guru culture, church leaders must repent of pride, bullying and exploitation, for "even the Son of Man did not come to be served, but to serve" (Mark 10:45).

To Elder-Pastor-Overseers who lead according to these principles, Peter offers this wonderful encouragement: "When the Chief Shepherd appears, you will receive the crown of glory" (1 Peter 5:4). How terrifying for neglectful pastors to stand before the Chief Shepherd having damaged any of his flock; but what joy to present them spiritually safe, healthy and well nourished, and to receive our crown of glory from Jesus, our perfect and eternal Elder-Pastor-Overseer.

Think it through

"Remember your leaders, who spoke the word of God to you. Consider the outcome of their way of life and imitate their faith ... Have confidence in your leaders and submit to their authority, because they keep watch over you as those who must give an account" (Hebrews 13:7, 17). Take time to pray for your Elder-Pastor-Overseers—that they would exercise pastoral ministry in the ways outlined in this chapter.

Church leaders: *Which of these areas of pastoral ministry most urgently need to be addressed in your church and your ministry, and how? Take time to pray for help to identify and rectify these weaknesses.*

14. Care for your local church

because it's very special to Jesus

"The church of God" Acts 20:28

If you look at the motley crew of ordinary, broken people who gather in most local churches, you might wonder why the Lord of heaven and earth would bother with us. Wouldn't he prefer something more impressive that reflects his glory and power? Wouldn't he want great crowds of A-list celebrities and successful superstars crammed into majestic cathedrals, stunning mega-churches and famous stadiums—a bit more like the Oscars or a Champions League Final or the Super Bowl?

Yet the Bible proclaims God's passionate love for your local church. For every church demonstrates the awesome power of God to accomplish his eternal plan to bring all things together under Christ through his reconciling death on the cross. However unimpressive the people, however painful the music, however tatty the building, our local congregation is a source of wonder in the heavenly realms and a miracle that prepares us for the spectacular multicultural festival which is the church of God in heaven.

For the heavenly church, expressed in countless earthly local churches, is Jesus' special project. When Peter first recognised that Jesus was the Christ, the Son of the living God, Jesus famously replied, "On this rock I will build my church, and the gates of Hades will not overcome it" (Matthew 16:18). From that conversation, we can see that every church *belongs* to Jesus, for he says, "I will build *my* church"; every church is being *built* by Jesus, for he promised, "I will *build* my church"; every church is founded on the *gospel* about Jesus, for he says, "On *this rock* I will build my church"; and every church is *preserved* by Jesus, for he reassures us, "The gates of Hades *will not* overcome it". Jesus is guaranteeing that the place of the dead will not be able to keep his people locked out of his heavenly church. But *why* was Jesus so determined to purchase, build, support and preserve his church?

Paul tells us more about the glory of Jesus' church in his letter to these Ephesians. He uses three glorious images of the church—as Jesus' *body, building* and *bride*:

Every church is the *body* of which Christ is the *head*

> "God placed all things under his feet and appointed him
> to be head over everything for the church."
>
> Ephesians 1:22

Christ has been appointed ruler or "head" over everything. Amazingly, Christ's dominion over the cosmos is "*for* the church". Paul describes the heavenly church, of which all believers are members, as a body of which Christ is the head (Ephesians 1:22-23). This has wonderful implications:

- **Christ rules his church as the head of the body**—Paul explains elsewhere that believers in a church are like limbs of a body with mutual responsibilities. Here he emphasises that Christ is the head, ruling the whole cosmos and his churches (including church leaders) for our spiritual benefit.

- **Christ unites the church in his body**—as the head was understood to be the inspiring, ruling, and guiding centre of unity for our human bodies, so Christ is the uniting ruler of every church. Speaking of Jesus' death, Paul says, "His purpose was to create in himself one new humanity out of the two, thus making peace, *and in one body to reconcile both of them to God through the cross*" (Ephesians 2:15-16). Christ's purpose in dying for our sins was to create in his church a new humanity—united in common dependence upon his death and destroying racial and social divisions, even between Jew and Gentile. The gospel of the cross (and not church leaders) is the means of unity within and between churches.

- **Christ shares his inheritance with his body**—the unity of Christians in church is far more than an enjoyable social occasion, for "through the gospel the Gentiles are heirs together with Israel, members together of one body" (Ephesians 3:6). Gentiles are grafted into the believing people of Israel as members of one body—sharing in blessings given in Christ (not in our church leaders).

The body imagery is used in Ephesians to emphasise that, above our church leaders, Christ rules us, unites us and shares with us in his body as members of his new human race—his church! So...

*The **challenge** of being his **body**
is to **preserve our unity.***

Despite our cultural and personal diversity, our unity in the body of Christ brings an obligation: "Make every effort to keep the unity of the Spirit through the bond of peace" (Ephesians 4:3); in other words, work at the practical co-operation in gospel work (not necessarily organisational unity) that expresses our spiritual unity in Christ. It is precisely because the selfishness of sin creates hostility and division that the power of God is evident in the harmony and co-operation of a local church. Indeed, Paul's letter to these Ephesians is his call to stand firm together in global mission despite Satan's efforts to inflame division (hence its climactic call to stand firm in God's armour of gospel convictions, Ephesians 6).

Every church is the *building* of which Christ is the *cornerstone*

Paul also describes the local church as the temple dwelling of the living God:

> "[God's] household, built on the foundation of the apostles and prophets, with Christ Jesus himself as the chief cornerstone. In him the whole building is joined together and rises to become a holy temple in the Lord. And in him you too are being built together to become a dwelling in which God lives by his Spirit."
>
> Ephesians 2:19-22

The greatest blessing of Adam and Eve in the Garden of Eden was to have God present to speak with them. The greatest blessing of Israel was to have the LORD dwelling with them— initially in a moveable tabernacle and later in Solomon's stunning temple in Jerusalem—to hear their prayers, forgive their sins and guide them with his law. When Israel was exiled to Babylon, the prophet Ezekiel promised a new and perfect temple from which God's blessing would flow like an ocean to the ends of the earth. This promise was fulfilled in Jesus who "tabernacled" among us (see "made his dwelling", John 1:14), whose body was God's "temple", destroyed by man but raised after three days (John 2:19).

Today, God continues to live with his people as his Holy Spirit indwells every Christian, making each of us "God's temple" (1 Corinthians 3:16; 6:19). And when Christians gather together in church, "we are the temple of the living God" (2 Corinthians 6:16). This glorious privilege is as true for a little church as a big one, because where even two or three are gathered in the name of Christ, he is in the midst of them. Every believer and every local church is home to the living God! Indeed, the word "household" describes the church as the family of God. God the Father has adopted us all in Christ as his sons and heirs: beloved, disciplined and protected by the Father, with constant access to him in prayer. And so we are to relate to each other in purity as brothers and sisters—treating older Christians with the loving deference due to parents, and treating younger Christians with the affection due to our own children. So...

*The **challenge** of being the **building of Christ** is to **grow in holiness**.*

The character of this family residence should be our Father's holiness—the unique, gracious purity of God's divine character. "In him [Christ] the whole building ... rises to become *a holy temple* in the Lord" (Ephesians 2:21). As one might move into a derelict and disgusting old building to gradually set about renovation and redecoration, so we are being renovated and redecorated spiritually by God on an "extreme makeover" scale. It should be the great concern of every Christian church not only to be united, but to work at being holy as our Father in heaven is holy.

Every church is the *bride* of which Christ is her *husband*

In teaching husbands and wives how to relate to each other, Paul explains that marriage, given by God as the bedrock for the continuation of human society, is modelled upon Christ's relationship with his church:

> "Wives, submit yourselves to your own husbands as you do to the Lord. For the husband is the head of the wife as Christ is the head of the church, his body, of which he is the Saviour ... Husbands, love your wives, just as Christ loved the church and gave himself up for her ... no one ever hated their own body, but they feed and care for their body, just as Christ does the church."
>
> Ephesians 5:22-29

It is clear that God has created the human covenant of marriage to help us understand the passionate commitment of Christ to his church in three ways:

- **Christ loves us**—in fact, he is so devoted to us that he sacrificed everything ("himself") to bring us to heaven to spiritually be "married" to him in loving and joyful intimacy, making us as spotless in his clean, holy and blameless life as any bride in her white wedding dress.

- **Christ provides what we need**—he "feeds and cares" for us as attentively as anyone would provide for their own body. We're to imagine how a caring husband will listen, understand and provide what his wife needs, to grasp how tenderly Jesus will always provide for us.

- **Christ is united intimately with us**—we are "members of his body" (v 30)—he goes wherever we go and knows how we feel, living and sharing life together with us. The union of a husband and wife spiritually, emotionally and sexually helps us understand how intimately Jesus knows us. Indeed, those who are unmarried in this life will not miss out—we will all experience in Christ an ecstatic intimacy in love of which even the best earthly marriage is only a pale reflection. So...

*The **challenge** of being the **bride of Christ** is to **submit to him.***

We are to respond to Christ's love as a wife is expected to respond to her husband, in glad submission: "Wives, submit yourselves to your own husbands ... as the church submits to Christ" (Ephesians 5:22, 24). Every Christian church is expected to gladly submit to the Word of Christ in Scripture, for he is our loving husband. This is most challenging when his words conflict with our cultural preferences, and we show our love for him by our trusting submission to the Bible.

These three beautiful images of every local church—the *body* of which Christ is the ruling head, the *building* of which Christ is the chief cornerstone, and the *bride* of which Christ is the loving husband—emphasise that Christ must be the centre of attention in every local church. For Jesus has publicly made his wedding vow...

I will build my church!

Think it through

1. *How has this chapter challenged or increased your valuation of your own church?*

2. *How healthy would your church be if everyone else shared your level of attendance, giving, love, commitment and prayerfulness?*

Church leaders: *What areas of unity, holiness and submission most urgently need to be addressed in your church—and how can this be done?*

15. Proclaim his death

because the blood of Christ has paid for us

"The church of God, which he bought with his own blood"
Acts 20:28

In Bible-teaching churches around the globe, the death of Christ is not just important but central. His bloody self-sacrifice is the supreme revelation of his transcendent glory, the pivotal moment in history, and the uniting focus of the Bible. Indeed, the "tree of life" that appears in descriptions of the Garden of Eden at the beginning of Scripture, and in the new creation at the end of Scripture, symbolises the wooden cross at the heart of Scripture!

We have observed before that in his body of the church, Christ is the head and his cross is the heart, pumping the lifeblood of his grace through all the teaching arteries of the church to keep the organs and limbs of his body alive. The death of Christ is indeed not just important—it is central to our Christian faith.

In just a few carefully selected words, Paul reminds these leaders of the very greatest doctrines of the cross when he describes the Ephesian church as "bought with his own blood". *Each word is pregnant with meaning.*

"Bought" means ransomed from slavery

The word "bought" is language from the slave-market. It refers to the ransom-price paid to free or "redeem" us from our slavery, our willing addiction to sin—whether in rebellion (such as pride and unbelief) or in idolatry (such as worshipping career and status, comfort and pleasure, family and security, or our own image and popularity). The Old Testament explanation of redemption is in Exodus 12, when the Israelites were slaves in Egypt.

God told his people to paint some blood from a sacrificed lamb over the doors of their homes to show that death for their sin had already occurred. This would satisfy God's justice and divert his wrath, which would "pass over" their firstborn sons. This Passover sacrifice "bought" the Israelites freedom from the judgment of God and slavery to Pharaoh. God did this to help us understand that Jesus was our Passover sacrifice, because his blood was shed instead of ours. As a lightning conductor attracts lightning bolts, Jesus diverted onto himself the lightning of God's wrath at our sin, so that we will survive his coming wrath, as heirs of heaven. He fully paid our ransom-price, not with cash but with his blood (his death). He bought us freedom from the miserable slavery of life under God's wrath, and from captivity to Satan's accusations and claims upon us under God's law. We're **free**—"bought" with his blood!

"Blood" means cleansing by his sacrifice

The word "blood" is language from the temple. In Leviticus 16, the significance of blood sacrifice is developed beyond that of the Passover in the climactic temple ceremony of the Day of Atonement. There, Israel's sin was regarded as a corrupting filthiness before God. The high priest would sacrifice a goat and offer its blood to God, showing that the punishment for the sin of the people had occurred. The high priest would then confess the people's sins over another goat and have it released into the desert to die (as the "scapegoat"). The Israelites were then regarded by God as pure and clean for living in his presence. This double sacrifice was designed to illustrate twin aspects of Jesus' death. Christ's blood has both satisfied God and taken away our guilt (technically called "propitiation" and "expiation", respectively) and we should celebrate both. When we rely on the blood of Jesus shed for our sin on the cross, God treats us as pure and clean for living with him. We're **clean**—"washed" by his blood!

"His own" means acceptable in him

The surprising words "his own blood" are literally "the blood of his own" and must refer, not to God bleeding (since he's spirit), but to Jesus, bleeding in completion of the perfect life that we haven't lived, to qualify us for heaven. This reference to God's own is probably alluding to God's "righteous servant", promised in words made famous by the music of Handel's *Messiah*, "pierced for our transgressions ... *my righteous servant will justify many*" (Isaiah 53:5, 11). (And even if there is no intended link to Isaiah here, this great truth of being justified by grace through faith in Christ is explained many times in Scripture, such as in Romans 3 – 5.)

This is law-court language, where our sin is understood as our failure to live righteously in obedience to God's law. Isaiah promises that God's own righteous servant will *justify many* because his righteous life was lived to qualify his people for God's approval—his "justification". When we trust in "the blood of his own" suffering servant, God declares us acceptable, or "justified", in *Christ's* righteousness, for living in the presence of God. Let me illustrate.

When I was invited recently to a "James Bond" birthday party in a smart country club, the men were required to wear "black tie" (dinner suits). I discovered to my horror that my own dinner jacket was filthy and damaged, and didn't fit me anymore! Thankfully, I was able to borrow my friend's clean, new dinner suit to get me into the party. To draw the serious parallel, we can't live with God, now or in heaven, unless we're righteous (holy like God). We're in big trouble because, however hard we try, we will never be righteous enough to be acceptable in God's presence. Thankfully, in his amazing grace, Jesus came to live the righteous and obedient life required from us, for us—and he completed it, covered in blood on that cross, with the triumphant cry, "It is finished". And we know for certain that his life does qualify us to live in God's presence, because Christ has already been resurrected and accepted into heaven (Romans 4:25)! When Paul speaks of the "blood of his own", he means the completed righteousness of Jesus that qualifies us for life in God's presence. We're **acceptable**—by his blood!

"Bought" means that payment was made for God's people on the cross

The words "bought with his own blood" also clearly mean that the ransom-price was paid for God's people when the blood was shed. This contains two wonderful truths.

First, this means that Jesus' death was for the *particular* people chosen by God for his heavenly church (sometimes called his "particular" or, less helpfully, "limited" atonement). Understandably, some worry that this sounds as if Jesus' death was somehow limited. Certainly not—the death of Christ our King was fully sufficient for all his people, however numerous! There's nothing limited about Jesus' death.

But it isn't true or helpful to say that Jesus died for everyone's sins (or why did Jesus teach that some will tragically face punishment in hell—which would be unnecessary and unjust if their punishment has already been suffered by Jesus on the cross?). Great theologians through the ages, such as John Owen in the seventeenth century and J.I. Packer in ours, have helpfully clarified how the Bible proclaims that, although no one deserves to be saved, Jesus died for all his people, but not all people. (Jesus confirms this in John 6:36-44. See also Acts 13:38-39; Ephesians 1:4-5; Romans 8:29-30.) Paul explains in Romans 9 that being chosen for this salvation should profoundly humble us.

Second, this means that our salvation was accomplished and secured by the death of Christ, and not achieved by our faith. We were completely ransomed by Jesus at the cross— so Jesus didn't die wondering if any of us would be smart enough to appreciate what he'd done. He hasn't been sitting in heaven biting his nails and hoping that we will decide to put our faith in him, or even waiting to see if his Spirit will be able to persuade us to do so. Once he died for us, the rest of our salvation has been inevitable. His death was *effective* in saving his people... on the cross!

Some have suggested that his death was "sufficient for all at the cross and effective to some through our faith". This sounds as if our salvation was uncertain until we put our faith in Christ. But Paul's word "bought" confirms that we were ransomed at the cross: our salvation was accomplished and secured by his death. Yes, this salvation is later applied to our experience by his Spirit calling us through the gospel to faith in him. But this has been certain ever since Jesus died. Everything that has contributed to our salvation since then is the result of his death for us. We're not saved because we have more faith than others, but because he died for us.

The golden thread running through all these wonderful aspects of Jesus' death is the simple and glorious *swap* that we never tire of proclaiming and celebrating. There are twin aspects to this beautiful exchange. Jesus was treated as if he were us and punished for our sin ("penal substitution") so that we can be treated as if we were him and accepted as sons into God's family ("justification by faith"). Indeed, it was rediscovering *both* sides of this swap that ignited the spiritual revival of the European Reformation and propelled the gospel around the globe.

Let me illustrate with the extraordinary heroism of Bill Deacon, the winchman of an Air-Sea Rescue helicopter operating in the Shetland Islands, northeast of the Scottish mainland. In November 1997, the *Green Lily* cargo vessel was grounded on rocks and breaking up in mountainous waves. The lifeboats could no longer get to the stricken vessel to save the crew trapped on board. Bill Deacon realised that the only hope of saving the men was to descend from the helicopter himself onto the ship. Once on the deck, in hurricane conditions, he attached each of the ten crew to his winch and, in his place, they were raised to safety. But as the last man was rescued, Bill Deacon himself was swept off the ship by a wave and his body was washed up a few days later. He was posthumously awarded the George Cross for his courage. He came down to swap places with each of the crew in the storm and died, so that the crew could take his place in the safety of the helicopter and live.

In the same way, Christ came down to swap places with us, not as a tragic victim but as a heroic volunteer, triumphantly accomplishing his Father's stunning plan. For despite our sin, God loves us more than we shall ever understand! For God to allow someone to swap places with us is grace; for God to provide that person is amazing grace; for God to be the person who swapped places with us on the cross is grace beyond measure! We're **saved**—by his blood shed on the cross!

So this tiny power-packed verse reminds us that we are...

- bought **free** from slavery to sin and judgment...
- **cleansed** from our corruption and guilt...
- **acceptable** to God in his perfect life...

and it was all accomplished on the **cross**!

We celebrate these fantastic truths every time we share the Lord's Supper, as Jesus commanded us to do in remembrance of him. Perhaps you can now see why the cross of Christ is not just important but central—the focus of our everlasting joy. It's because there we were "bought with his own blood"!

Think it through

1. *Which aspects of Christ's death for you do you find most exciting and why?*

2. *Is there a Bible passage about the death of Jesus that has particularly impacted you in the past?*

3. *How would you explain "the swap" in language that would make sense to an unbeliever? Or to a child?*

Church leaders: *Are all these aspects of the death of Christ given sufficiently clear explanation and emphasis in your church?*

16. Beware of the wolves

because distorted teaching savages churches

"I know that after I leave, savage wolves will come in among you and will not spare the flock. Even from your own number men will arise and distort the truth in order to draw away disciples after them. So be on your guard! Remember that for three years I never stopped warning each of you night and day with tears." Acts 20:29-31

I once watched a pack of wolves rip a carcass apart in a game park. The wolves had been lazily dozing on a rocky outcrop when a park warden threw the body of a deer into the other end of the enclosure. Suddenly, the wolves were alert; they sniffed the scent and sprang to their feet. Silently, the whole pack loped off with deceptive speed in the direction of the meat, some taking a high path and others the lower path. Arriving together, the wolves fell upon the carcass and tore it to bits. It was disturbing to watch such measured savagery.

Paul says that's what false teachers can do spiritually to our churches. Paul wasn't so worried by those who flatly *deny* the truth—like atheists or Muslims today. He warns these Ephesians about those who *distort* the truth, misusing Christian language to teach something unbiblical. Even these Elders could be deceived, or themselves become dangerous, if they allowed themselves to be driven by a yearning for influence to teach popular distortions. Like Jesus before him, Paul warns that twisted interpretations of Scripture are not interesting alternatives but savagely destructive of saving faith.

Our culture doesn't like negativity—and the Bible teaches us to respect people and not to be arrogant or argumentative. But as children need loving parental warnings about dangerous roads or drugs, young Christians need protection from damaging error. Paul took no pleasure in this. He warned these Ephesians "with tears", heartbroken at discovering the lies and exploitation of false teachers. Of course, none of us understand or teach Scripture perfectly. And Christians will always debate and disagree about secondary details of doctrine, such as creation, baptism or prophecy. But because people's salvation is at stake, we must "contend for the faith" with those who distort the gospel, such as "ungodly people, who pervert the grace of our God into a licence for immorality and deny Jesus Christ" (Jude 4), or those claiming, contrary to 1 Corinthians 6:9-11, that unrepentant sexual immorality will not exclude us from God's kingdom.

Indeed, most New Testament letters contain warnings against false teaching. Sometimes, this was distortion of the religious kind—*adding* human traditions to biblical faith, like pressure to observe Jewish laws (Galatians 6:12-16), or pressure to accept the human ideology, religious observance and visionary experiences of the false teachers (Colossians 2:8, 16, 18). In other letters, the false teaching was of the liberal kind—*subtracting* culturally unpopular aspects of biblical teaching, such as that God became man (1 John 4:1-3). All false teaching is fuelled by Satan, the "father of lies", and is defeated by the Spirit of truth through sound teaching.

Other religions will sometimes prey upon unbelievers by claiming to teach the Bible (as Jehovah's Witnesses and Mormons do). More dangerous to Christian believers is distortion that claims to be Christian. In every age since Christ, different aspects of biblical Christianity have been attacked. Faithful responses to these challenges help clarify what is distinctive about "Reformed evangelical" (that is, biblical) faith:

- In the first three centuries of Christianity, *the divinity of Christ* was attacked (our distinctive view of *Jesus*), and defended by champions like Athanasius against heretics like Arius.

- In the fourth and fifth centuries, it was *the seriousness of sin* (our distinctive view of *humanity*), defended by champions like Augustine against heretics like Pelagius.

- In the Middle Ages in Europe, it was *Jesus' substitutionary death*: that is, Christ dying in our place to satisfy God so that we can be saved (our distinctive view of *the cross*)— championed by men like Anselm against those, later led by Abelard, who taught that salvation is won through our own moral living inspired by Jesus.

- By the 16th century, it was *justification by grace through faith alone* (our distinctive view of *salvation*), rediscovered and defended by champions like Luther and Zwingli despite Catholic persecution.

- In 17th-century Europe, it was *the sovereignty of God* in salvation (our distinctive view of *God*) being defended by champions like Calvin against those, later led by Arminius, who wrongly emphasised human free will in salvation.

- In the "Puritan" age in England in the 17th century, it was the need for *regeneration* (our distinctive view of the *Holy Spirit*), defended by heroes like Owen and Baxter against High Anglicanism.

- In the 18th-century revivals in Britain and the US, it was the reality of *the coming judgment* (our distinctive view of *history*), preached by Whitfield, Wesley and Edwards against the liberals.

- In the 19th century, it was the *urgency of mission* (our distinctive view of the *world*), championed by men like Hudson Taylor in China, William Carey in India, and C.T. Studd in Africa against selfish "Reformed" apathy.

- At the beginning of the 20th century, it was the authority of *Scripture* (our distinctive view of the *Bible*), defended by men like Warfield and Machen against liberal scholars from theological colleges.

- By the middle of the 20th century, it was *the centrality of expository preaching* in the local church (our distinctive view of *ministry*), defended by Lloyd-Jones, Stott and Lucas against the social priorities of the ecumenical movement.

- At the end of the 20th century, it was *the primacy of the local congregation* being attacked (our distinctive view of the *church*), and defended by champions like Broughton Knox and Phillip Jensen against the centralism of Western denominations.

- As we begin the 21st century, the false teaching tearing apart established denominations is that challenging the necessity of *repentance from sin* for salvation (our distinctive view of *holiness*), which is contrary to the hedonism of personal autonomy. This is now morphing into a challenge to the *"given-ness" of our gender* by God (our distinctive view of *creation*), and we await the emergence of our theological champions.

But perhaps the most familiar and widespread distortion of biblical faith over many centuries has been Roman Catholicism. Indeed, many reading this may be shocked to think of Roman Catholicism as false teaching! Clearly, some Roman Catholic teaching is faithful to Scripture and many Catholics don't believe everything taught by the Pope or the Vatican. Some have clearly been born again through believing the gospel despite what they hear. But, tragically, the distinctive doctrines of Roman Catholicism are a serious distortion of biblical faith. And those converted from a Catholic background keep urging me to be more forthright in exposing the dangerous errors taught every week in Catholic schools and churches around the world. So let me outline some core Roman Catholic beliefs (those readily available in the Roman Catholic Shorter Catechism) to ensure that you are not misled.

Error 1: Christ is not enough

Tragically, Rome teaches that Christ is inadequate to save us. Rome teaches that Christ is not sufficient as our mediator in heaven by *adding* mediators—and not sufficient in his sacrificial death on the cross by *adding* the sacrifice of the mass.

The additional mediators are priests, saints and Mary. Rome teaches people to confess their sins to a priest (at "confession") to obtain forgiveness ("absolution"), and to pray to dead "saints" to influence God. But when English Bibles say that our heavenly Father hears "the prayers of the saints", this means the prayers of genuine believers and not, say, "Our Lady of Fatima". Further, the veneration of "relics" (bones of saints) is just pagan superstition.

Above all, Rome teaches people to pray to Mary saying, "Hail Mary, full of grace ... pray for us now and at the hour of our death"; that is, asking her to save us by her grace. Catholics are taught that Mary is a new Eve (parallel with Jesus as the new Adam), our Mother (parallel with God our Father), our "Mediatrix" and "Co-Redemptrix" (parallel with Jesus as our Mediator and Redeemer), and Queen of heaven (parallel to Christ as our King)! To teach that Jesus shares these glorious roles with another, even his godly but imperfect mother, is truly dreadful. (Mary is regarded as "full of grace" to save us because of a misinterpretation of Luke 1:28, where she's described as "highly favoured".) Roman Catholic teaching about priests, saints and Mary diminishes Christ and offers powerless mediators. The Bible says, "There is one God and one mediator between God and mankind, the man Christ Jesus" (1 Timothy 2:5).

The additional sacrifice for sins is "the mass". Rome treats Jesus' death as inadequate because it also requires the "mass" (the Roman Catholic version of "holy communion") as a sacrifice for sins to God (to "re-present" his death). Catholics are taught that the bread and wine become spiritually the body and blood of Jesus offered on an altar by a priest to satisfy God. Any leftover bread and wine must either be eaten by the priest or "reserved" in a box as sacred.

But the Bible teaches that the "Lord's Supper" recalls and commemorates the completed satisfaction of God regarding payment for our sins at the cross (looking back), participates in the risen Jesus by faith (looking up), anticipates the great feast in the new creation (looking forward), and appreciates all who eat and drink in dependence on Christ's death (looking around). The essential difference is that Rome thinks the direction of the mass is towards God as *a sacrifice*, but the Bible teaches that the direction of the Lord's Supper is towards us as *an illustration*. The mass is a truly dreadful denial of the finished work of Christ on the cross. Christ is triumphant in heaven and not dead on the table, for the Bible says, "After he had provided purification for sins, he sat down at the right hand of the Majesty in heaven" (Hebrews 1:3).

Error 2: Scripture is not enough

Tragically, Rome teaches that Scripture is inadequate, and so Christians must obey both the Bible and the teachings of the church (the Pope and his bishops) for salvation. For example, look at this extraordinarily candid statement:

> *"The church ... does not derive her certainty about all revealed truths from the Holy Scriptures alone. Both Scripture and Tradition must be accepted and honoured with equal sentiments of devotion and reverence."*
> Roman Catholic Catechism, paragraph 82

But Scripture says there's only one light of revelation, which is the Bible: "You will do well to pay attention to it, as to a light shining in a dark place" (2 Peter 1:19).

Unfortunately, Roman Catholicism adds to Scripture not only the books of the "Apocrypha" (ancient writings like "Bel and the Dragon", which don't have an Apostle of Jesus as their source), but also the declarations of the Pope and decisions of his councils of bishops.

Moreover, Rome says that only the Pope and his bishops can understand the Bible:

> *"The task of interpreting the Word of God authentically has
> been entrusted solely to the Magisterium of the Church,
> that is to the Pope and to the Bishops in communion with
> him."* Roman Catholic Catechism, paragraph 100

But Scripture says that the Holy Spirit helps ordinary believers to understand his Word: "Reflect on what I am saying, for the Lord will give you insight into all this" (2 Timothy 2:7).

These statements open the door to all kinds of distortions; for example, it was finally decided in the fifth century that Mary was perpetually a virgin, despite the Gospels' references to Joseph consummating his marriage and to Jesus' brothers and sisters (Matthew 1:25; Mark 3:31, 6:3); in 1854 Pope Pius IX declared that Mary was immaculate (sinless) from conception; and in 1950 Pope Pius XII declared that Mary didn't die but was taken, or "assumed", bodily into heaven. These statements rest on so-called "papal infallibility"—a perfection that belongs only to God's words in Scripture.

Error 3: Faith is not enough

Rome claims to teach that we're saved by grace, but grace is regarded as power from God received through seven "sacraments" (signs) of the church, to help us become good enough for heaven. These are baptism (thought to give automatic salvation to babies), confirmation, confession, the mass, priesthood, marriage and holy unction (absolution just before death). But the Bible says God's saving grace is not what God does *in* us but what God has done *for* us in Christ (and Scripture gives only two signs of the gospel—baptism and the Lord's Supper).

To remove the imperfections in us when we die, Rome says we must suffer in "purgatory". This time in purgatory is said to be reduced by prayers (symbolised by candles in church) and "indulgences" (reductions in suffering paid for in money or service) from the Pope. For example, here is an extract from of 2013 when the Pope offered indulgences to young people who attended a Catholic "Youth Day" in Rio:

> *"Pope Francis decreed that World Youth Day participants can receive one plenary, or full, indulgence a day if they meet the usual conditions ... An indulgence is a remission of the temporal punishment a person is due for sins that have been forgiven. The conditions necessary for receiving a plenary indulgence include having recently gone to confession, receiving the Eucharist and offering prayers for the intentions of the pope."*
>
> Catholic News Service, "Vatican Announces Indulgences for World Youth Day" (accessed 22/12/16)

But the thief to whom Christ said, "Today you will be with me in paradise" (Luke 23:43) certainly had not bought an indulgence! Paul clarifies:

> "We believe that God will bring with Jesus those who have fallen asleep in him."   1 Thessalonians 4:14

Christians are safe with the Lord until the resurrection, and certainly not suffering in purgatory.

Tragically, and most fundamentally, the Roman church ignores the great gospel truth of "justification by grace through *faith alone*". This was rediscovered by Martin Luther and the Reformers in the Reformation and is encapsulated in these words from Paul about the *swap* proclaimed in the gospel:

> "God made him who had no sin [i.e. Jesus] to be sin for us [i.e. on the cross], so that in him [i.e. by faith] we might become the righteousness of God [i.e. acceptable in heaven]."   2 Corinthians 5:21

We are not saved by God's Spirit giving *us* grace through church sacraments to become good enough for heaven. We are saved by Jesus completing the perfect life required of a Christian that qualifies us for heaven. We are not saved by Christ's righteousness being *imparted* by his Spirit into us, but by the righteousness of Christ being *imputed* and counted to all who believe in him. We are not saved by God's grace in *us* but in *Christ!*

There is a mystifying willingness of some supposedly-biblical churches to partner with Roman Catholic churches in mission. But what our Roman Catholic friends urgently need—like other religious people trying to be good enough for heaven—is to hear God's spectacular gospel. This proclaims, as the great 16th-century Reformers discovered, salvation in Christ alone, by grace alone, through faith alone, according to Scripture alone, to the glory of God alone. Indeed, many Roman Catholics are eager to discuss these things, because they live under terrible burdens of guilt and fear.

Don't be afraid or naive. For Paul said, "Be on your guard!"

Think it through

1. *How would you answer someone who said that we should not say anything negative about what other people teach?*

2. *Why do you think false teachers who claim to be Christian are in many ways more dangerous than atheist writers?*

3. *Most of us will have Roman Catholic friends or family. How could we gently challenge their faith in Mary, the mass, the Pope and the sacraments, and get them to discuss what the Bible says?*

Church leaders: *How can you ensure that the saving "swap" of justification by grace through faith is offered to every unbeliever?*

17. Trust God

because he is utterly magnificent

"Now I commit you to God." Acts 20:32

Paul could leave these inexperienced leaders running a baby church because he trusted God to look after them. For God is utterly magnificent and worthy of our complete trust and delight. Let me celebrate God with you a little...

If we ask, "What is God like?" we're stuck because God is **unique in his transcendent glory**. he can't be compared with anything or anyone else. Thankfully, God has graciously revealed himself to us so that we can enjoy him. And he has explained that his eternal plan is to prepare for his Son an adoring bride, a vast multicultural church spectacularly saved and transformed by his grace to glorify and enjoy him for ever. He created the universe to display his magnificence. He scripted world history as the divine playwright writing himself into the action with the biggest part. He then employed Old Testament Prophets and New Testament Apostles to testify to his Son in the Bible, which climaxed in him taking flesh to die for our sins and rising to rule. And he created us according to his image in God the Son, so that when his Son condensed himself down as one of us in Jesus, he lived and spoke in categories that we can understand in the Bible.

Here, God is revealed and celebrated in mind-blowing descriptions of his character, attributes, names, works, glory, contrasts and, above all, in countless reasons to praise him. His Spirit not only calls us through this text but indwells us to enlighten our minds and hearts—not just to understand or experience God, but to regenerate us to know him personally! Here are some of his most captivating attributes:

God is personal: relational

He is distinct from his creation, free, intelligent, self-conscious and affectionate. Being personal he is self-aware, so he can make himself known to us; he makes personal decisions and plans to do what he wills for his glory; and so he establishes personal relationships with us in which he speaks personally to us in the words of Scripture and listens to us responding in personal words of prayer.

God is spirit: uncontainable

He's not made of anything. He's without body or form. He's invisible, immeasurable, uncontrollable and without need or weakness.

God is infinite: the origin and purpose of everything

All things come from him (he's the origin of everything), all things are through him (he sustains everything), and all things are to him (he steers everything for his ultimate glory, in which we find delight).

God is Trinity: three in one

There is only one living God and he is three persons in one, each distinct but not separate, and united but not fused. The Bible never speaks of three Gods or God in three forms. Each person of the Trinity is equally God, but they are ordered, for God the Father exercises loving authority over God the Son and God the Holy Spirit, and the Spirit and Son lovingly submit to the Father—without undermining their equality or unity.

God is immanent: he is here

God is said by theologians to be "immense"—that is, he doesn't occupy space and he is not in created matter. Although he can reveal himself in particular locations like the burning bush, he's not confined to any location—whether in a temple or even in heaven, nor is he ever stretched across distance. God is "omnipresent" in that all of his being is personally present everywhere simultaneously, not by multiplying or dividing himself but by being completely everywhere. Indeed, nothing in the universe exists except by God's personal presence to sustain and govern it. God's centre is everywhere but his circumference is nowhere. He is our real environment, keeping us alive until he decides we must die. However, God is present differently in different places. God can make himself present to bless in Jesus and in heaven, or present to discipline his children, or present to punish his enemies in hell.

God is immutable: unchanging and reliable in his character, will and promises

God cannot change. If he could, he would be imperfect either before or after that change—and in either case he wouldn't be God! The great Westminster Shorter Catechism says, "God is a spirit, whose being, wisdom, power, holiness, justice, goodness, and truth are infinite, eternal, and unchangeable". Scripture teaches, for example:

> "God is not human, that he should lie, not a human
> being, that he should change his mind. Does he speak
> and then not act? Does he promise and not fulfil?"
>
> Numbers 23:19

God's immutability is of great comfort to us in approaching him and trusting his promises, especially his gospel. People change constantly because we are never perfect—so human nature is inherently unstable (with fickle emotions and weak characters) and untrustworthy (we are all hurt by infidelity of different kinds in people we have trusted). But God never changes. He's never unreliable in his words and promises, never unstable or inconsistent—he never leaves us uncertain about what he wants or how he will react.

So he is the **solid rock** on which we can build our lives in confidence; as Jesus said, "Everyone who hears these words of mine and puts them into practice is like a wise man who built his house on the rock" (Matthew 7:24). He is the **impregnable fortress** in whom we can seek refuge for safety, help and comfort: "The LORD is my rock, my fortress and my deliverer; my God is my rock, in whom I take refuge" (Psalm 18:2). Where we read in the Bible of God answering a prayer or showing compassion in not bringing destruction upon wicked people, it may sound as if he changes his mind. But he doesn't. He is reliably keeping his promises elsewhere to relent from sending punishment upon those who repent, and he has always planned to act when people pray—which encourages us to depend prayerfully upon him.

God is great

Psalm 139 proclaims that God is *all-knowing* (omniscient), so the writer says, *You know everything about me* (v 1-6); *ever-present* (omnipresent), so he says, *You are always with me* (v 7-12); and *all-powerful* (omnipotent) so he says, *You made every part of me* (v 13-18)! He is great beyond adequate description.

God is good

Psalm 145 emphasises that God is unbelievably good. He's *gracious* in his mighty works of creation and redemption (v 3-7), *wise* in his kingly rule over his people (v 8-13), *faithful* to all he has made in keeping his promises (v 13-16), and *righteous* in loving his people by sending our Saviour (v 17-20).

God is gracious

In Psalm 103, the psalm-writer offers an A-Z of reasons to praise the LORD, collected under three aspects of his character. He's our *beneficial Saviour,* who forgives and heals, redeems and loves, satisfies and renews us (v 2-5)! He's our *merciful Redeemer,* who works righteousness and justice for the oppressed, made his ways and deeds known to his people, is "compassionate and gracious, slow to anger, abounding in love", and removes our transgressions as far as the east is from the west (v 6-12)! And he's our *everlasting Father,* who shows compassion to all who fear him, and knows that we're formed of dust and will wither like flowers. Yet from everlasting to everlasting the LORD's love is with all who fear him (v 13-19)!

God is impassible: not obliged to do anything but voluntarily loves to

God's "impassibility" is his freedom from being subject to pain or any emotion caused by another. God is completely self-sufficient (this is his "aseity"), so he doesn't need anything. But his self-sufficiency doesn't mean he can't volunteer to suffer or feel compassion. God cannot suffer any damage to his own divine attributes or character—but he has from eternity voluntarily accepted the pain and grief of loving revoltingly wicked sinners like us. In fact, in Jesus, God the Son even took flesh to suffer for us, while God the Father suffered loss and grief in giving up his beloved Son. But Jesus was never the victim of our need, nor of the Father's plan. Jesus voluntarily gave himself for us on the cross—in love!

God is "simple": maximally alive

In admiring different aspects of God's goodness, we must respect his "simplicity"—that he is all of his qualities, all of the time, because he is personal. He can act differently towards different people and in different circumstances, just as a fire may bring comforting warmth or helpful light or terrifying destruction! But he is unchanging in his perfections. So we can't interpret one attribute of his character as contradicting another; therefore, when we teach that God is love, we must remember that he is still holy and just to judge. When we teach that he sovereignly allows us to suffer to learn to be like Jesus, we must remember that he is still being loving. As a prism reveals different elements in light, the Bible reveals different aspects of God, but he's always the same unchanging God—"maximally alive" in all his wonderful attributes at the same time.

God took flesh: Jesus

God's gospel proclaims that Jesus is this God—fully man and fully God, one man with two natures, full of grace and truth (John 1:14-18).

God is glorious: our supreme delight

The 17th-century Westminster Confession famously declares, "The chief end of man is to glorify God and enjoy him for ever". In his beautiful book *Desiring God*, John Piper explains that this always meant "to glorify God *by* enjoying him". So Piper concludes in words of enormous significance that "God is most glorified when we are most satisfied in him". As football crowds enjoy roaring their devotion to their team, God's people love to sing God's praises, and to live and speak in ways that highlight his magnificence. And our joy in God is most satisfying when we can express our praises—*to him* in prayer and song, and *to others* in teaching and evangelism.

When we marvel and delight in God, he receives the glory he deserves and we find satisfaction in him. It's not that God is proud. Indeed, astonishing as it sounds, his glory is most brilliantly revealed in Jesus, in being humiliated and bleeding to death on the cross! He wants us to learn to praise him, not because he needs it but because we do—for it will bring us the happiness we were created to yearn for and an intoxicating taste of heaven.

When we reflect on some of the attributes we have just considered, we realise that, as Nehemiah reminded God's people, "the joy of the LORD is [our] strength" (Nehemiah 8:10)—and, like Paul, we can gladly entrust those we love to his care... because God is utterly magnificent!

Think it through

1. *How do you feel when you read these amazing things about God?*

2. *How central is the idea of knowing and enjoying God to your idea of heaven?*

3. *Read one of the psalms mentioned above and praise God for what it reveals of his character.*

Church leaders: *What will it mean for you to commit your church to God?*

18. Trust God's Word

to build people up

"Now I commit you to God and to the word of his grace,
which can build you up" Acts 20:32

Paul could leave the baby Ephesian church in the care of these inexperienced leaders because he could entrust them into the safekeeping of God and his Word, which builds up his people. We have considered the magnificence of God; now we can consider the power of his Word. That Word is dynamic:

"The word of God is alive and active."   Hebrews 4:12

The Bible is *alive* because the living Spirit of God speaks and empowers its text today. It's *active* because, as our own breath carries our words, so God's Spirit carries forth God's words in the Bible with compelling spiritual power. Indeed, as God spoke creation into existence, and as Jesus commanded the dead to come to life, so his Spirit continues to create new life in sinners and build up his church through the words of Scripture because they are invested with his divine personal authority. Christ promised to build his church (Matthew 16:18), and it is through his Word that he builds it.

More particularly, Paul says that "The word of his grace ... can build you up". This clarifies that it is the Bible taught with the gospel of God's grace in Christ as its central theme that builds his church. It is tragically possible for a church to claim to respect the Bible, but to be so selective or manipulative in order to be politically correct that God's grace is twisted until no one is saved or built up. In Western churches, God's grace is usually distorted not by teachers avoiding the truth that God loves us (which Westerners find obvious), but by them avoiding the accompanying truth that human beings are wicked and deserve God's judgment (which Westerners find ridiculous). By this distortion, God's grace in Christ's death is disregarded as unnecessary and unexceptional—and the church will not grow. Where the gospel of God's grace in saving hell-deserving sinners is taught from Scripture, Christ will build his church.

Indeed, I've spent the last 25 years employed in gospel ministry watching God do exactly this. He has grown our church and our church-planting movement in London through Bible-teaching of many kinds. So, when we celebrated our silver jubilee, our music director wrote a beautiful tribute to God's work among us, appropriately called, "Behold the power of his Word!" Although people who join us may say they were attracted not just by the teaching but by the warmth of the welcome or the quality of the children's work or the clarity of the mission or the joy of the praises, it is God's Word that generated those things. Paul later reminds Timothy (who became pastor of the church in Ephesus) of what is so amazing about the Bible, to encourage him to keep preaching it despite the cost of doing so:

> "The Holy Scriptures ... are able to make you wise for
> salvation through faith in Christ Jesus. All Scripture
> is God-breathed and is useful for teaching, rebuking,
> correcting and training in righteousness, so that the
> servant of God may be thoroughly equipped for every
> good work."   2 Timothy 3:15-17

When Paul referred to the "Holy Scriptures", the New Testament hadn't yet been written. He was speaking initially of the Old Testament, which Jesus regarded as God's words. But this category of "Holy Scriptures" would eventually include the New Testament, which was still being written, document by document, by Christ's Apostles, empowered by his Holy Spirit to remember "all things" taught them by Jesus (John 14:26).

It's important to know that documents were only accepted by the early churches as books of the Bible if they were both "apostolic" (meaning an Apostle who witnessed Christ's ministry was the author or source of the book) and "prophetic" (meaning consistent with the theological character of the Old Testament). So what Paul writes here is true of both Old and New Testaments (but not of the strange books of the "Apocrypha", which aren't apostolic).

Now, there are billions of books available today. When selecting a book to read, we normally consider the subject *(Does it matter?)*, the author *(Are they reliable?)* and the purpose of the book *(What benefit is there in reading it?)*. In these verses, Paul answers all three questions about the Bible.

The Bible is all about salvation through Christ: *a vital subject*

> "... able to make you wise for salvation through faith in
> Christ Jesus."   2 Timothy 3:15

The Bible is all about *Christ Jesus*—for Jesus said, "These are the very Scriptures that testify about me" and, when he rose from the dead, he explained himself in a Bible study saying, "Everything must be fulfilled that is written about me in the Law of Moses, the Prophets and the Psalms" (John 5:39, Luke 24:44). And...

The Bible is all about *salvation* from Satan, sin and hell for joy in the presence of God. And...

The Bible is also all about salvation *by faith* in the gospel promise (even back in Genesis, when the promise of the kingdom to Abram was very simple).

It was never good advice about what we must do for God, but good news about what God has done for us. It's not that every verse mentions salvation by faith in Christ, but that every verse contributes to our understanding of it.

So churches that don't just use the Bible, but listen to what God is saying in the text, will be churches where people are regularly being saved through faith in Christ.

The Bible is by God: *a reliable author*

"All Scripture is God-breathed."   2 Timothy 3:16

Reading the Bible is a scary business because God is speaking the text and judging how we respond to his voice in our hearts...

"Sharper than any double-edged sword, it [the Word] penetrates even to dividing soul and spirit, joints and marrow; it judges the thoughts and attitudes of the heart."   Hebrews 4:12

God uses his Word as a surgeon uses a scalpel to cut open someone's heart on an operating table. This is a blessing—for by judging us now through his Word, God performs his spiritual surgery upon us to prepare us for the judgment to come. For the words of God are always true and speak with final authority in correcting our faith and conduct. Jesus answers his opponents by quoting from Exodus saying, "Have you not read what God said to you, 'I am the God of Abraham...?'" (Matthew 22:31-32). He regards an ancient Old Testament text from Exodus as God's contemporary voice with decisive authority in his own day—like a text message from God, recorded long ago but personal and decisive today.

Of course, whatever God says must be important because he is our Creator, who designed us, and our Redeemer who loves us! And since he always speaks the truth with no reason to lie, whatever his text says (when responsibly interpreted) is completely "inerrant" (without error in all it affirms) and "infallible" (without mistakes except by literary convention, such as rounding up numbers or reporting events as they appear rather than scientifically, so that readers in every age can understand the language).

All the decisive guidance we need from God for our lives is found in the Bible—sometimes in theological principles, sometimes in exemplary characters, and sometimes in proverbial wisdom. God nowhere suggests that we attempt to negotiate any system of additional signs from him rather than simply accepting his word. Even where the Bible doesn't specifically tell me what to do, I can trust that God is sovereign, looking after me and steering my circumstances to help me become like Jesus.

Churches that listen to their Bibles will have a contemporary relationship with the living God, hearing his Spirit guiding them clearly through his Word.

The Bible is for righteousness: *an eternal benefit!*

> " ... useful for teaching, rebuking, correcting and training
> in righteousness." 2 Timothy 3:16

The Bible is for living and not just for admiration, education or quotation. The Bible is not for academic conquest. God is not impressed if we know the themes or structure of a Bible book. Since he wrote it, he wants us to live by it. And in Psalm 19, David describes the rich spiritual benefits of living by Scripture:

> "The law of the LORD is perfect, refreshing the soul. The
> statutes of the LORD are trustworthy, making wise the
> simple. The precepts of the LORD are right, giving joy to
> the heart. The commands of the LORD are radiant, giving
> light to the eyes. The fear of the LORD is pure, enduring
> for ever. The decrees of the LORD are firm, and all of
> them are righteous. They are more precious than gold,
> than much pure gold; they are sweeter than honey, than
> honey from the honeycomb. By them your servant is
> warned; in keeping them there is great reward."
>
> Psalm 19:7-11

The Bible is served by teachers. Although God's Word and God's Spirit are strictly all that we need, God in his mercy provides us with gifted and learned teachers. It's very striking that, having told Timothy that all Scripture is "useful for teaching, rebuking, correcting and training in righteousness" (3:16), Timothy is then told in similar language to...

> "... preach the word ... correct, rebuke and encourage—
> with great patience and careful instruction."
>
> 2 Timothy 4:2

God provides Bible teachers to serve the purpose of his Word. When we gather in church, the reason that we don't just hand out Bibles to read in silence is that teachers are helpful for explaining the Word and its necessary implications in language the congregation can understand. (As we noted in an earlier chapter, the local teacher is usually more helpful than a great preacher beamed onto a screen, because he knows the people and their context.)

All this means that Scripture is completely sufficient—it contains all we need to know from God to be...

"... thoroughly equipped for every good work."

2 Timothy 3:17

A preacher like Timothy, and any church listening to their teaching, has in the Bible everything they need to know from God to be fully equipped for every good work we could want to do for him. The Bible is like a Swiss army knife for a Christian—it has everything you could ever need. This is called the "sufficiency" of Scripture.

In summary, we have learnt that God's Word is **actively saving** (because it's all about salvation through faith in Christ), **reliably authoritative** (because God is speaking the truth and judging our responses) and **comprehensively sufficient** (because it trains us in righteousness for every good work).

Finally, it's helpful to understand that Jesus plainly understood the Spirit of God to be speaking *the meaning of the words on the pages of Scripture*. It's not in the oral sound or visual shape of the words (which are different in every language that God speaks), but in the plain original *meaning* of the words. So let's now clarify where God is not speaking:

- *God is not speaking in bad translations or additional notes and scholarly commentary.*

- *God is not speaking only in past original events,* leaving us (as "liberal" cynics suggest) to struggle to understand the flawed and outdated reports of gullible Bible witnesses. So Hebrews, for example, introduces numerous Old Testament texts by saying that God or Jesus or the Holy Spirit speaks them today (e.g. Hebrews 2:12; 3:7).

- *God is not speaking in the different interpretations generated by our hearts*—as if he says different things to different people. Of course, he speaks many things in every text, and different things will feel precious or challenging to different people, but what he is saying to everyone is still the words of the text (which means we can't invent what we want to hear, but can be held to account by the words of the Bible text). For God hasn't just given us a book to stimulate an independent relationship with himself. Rather, he speaks through the words of the text to maintain his relationship with his children;

- *God is not trying and failing to guide us with signs.* When preachers speak of hearing God's guidance from the Bible, from sanctified common sense, from the godly advice of friends and from the inner promptings of the Holy Spirit, they should mean that these are the different ways we discover what the Bible says! For the only way we know whether the common sense we hear is sanctified rather than worldly, or whether the advice we're given is godly and not sinful, or that promptings within us are the Holy Spirit reminding us of God's Word and not the temptations of Satan, is to check whether the Bible says it! If God wants to speak from a bush or write on a wall with a human hand as he has before (Exodus 3:4; Daniel 5:24), he can do so. The reason that he usually doesn't do so is that God's fully sufficient guidance is now given to us in his completed Bible.

- *God is not usually speaking in the dreams and messages that many claim are prophecy.* According to Acts 2, all believers are prophesying when, like Peter, we proclaim from the Scriptures the wonders of the Lord done in Jesus. Paul's writing about the gift of prophecy (1 Corinthians 14; Revelation 19:10) reminds us that spontaneous insights into Scripture come from God, and should be heard if they've been tested by those with a teaching office and judged as coming from the Bible—such gifts of prophetic insight into Scripture are well-evidenced in our various Bible studies, where some are gifted in contributing spontaneous insights given by God.

One persuasive piece of evidence for the enduring authority, vitality, clarity and sufficiency of Scripture is that on mid-week evenings, in churches across London, you will find thousands of young people who could be out socialising, carefully studying the Bible and finding it irresistibly persuasive! Intelligent people who hotly debate competing political ideologies, quickly diagnose errors in business proposals and contracts, and refuse to be taken in for a moment by the cleverest media marketing campaigns, gladly accept the truth of every word they read in the Bible! There's no other book like that!

We are convinced of the glorious *authority, vitality, sufficiency* and *clarity* of the Bible for all our lives and ministries, because the Bible is the Word of God!

Think it through

1. Does your attitude to God's Word, in the time you make to listen to God's Word and in how you respond when his Word says hard things, reflect the glories of God's Word?

2. Which parts of the Bible are you least familiar with? What do you think might be the result if you never read and study those parts?

3. Why do people so readily accept messages from beyond the Bible as being from God?

Church leader: How can you ensure that the Bible really is functioning as the sufficient and vital authority in your church?

19. Celebrate our inheritance

and enjoy the hope of heaven

"An inheritance among all those who are sanctified."
Acts 20:32

Someone from our Korean congregation was telling us recently about the dreadful persecution of Christians in North Korea. As I mentioned more briefly in chapter 4, in an attempt to enforce abject submission to the will of the state, our brothers and sisters in Christ have been used for testing biological weapons, shipped off to death camps, had their newborn children despicably tortured, and their leaders pulverized in the street with steamrollers. I am told that as they lay down for the steamroller to be driven over their heads in front of their distraught families, they were singing an old song about heaven: "Nearer, my God, to Thee".

Closer to home, a friend recently told me about the death of his father. Both of his parents were mature believers in Christ, and both in their nineties. My friend sensed that his father, extremely weak and close to death, was fighting for life for fear of hurting his mother. He suggested to her that she could, as it were, give him permission to go. She agreed and by his bedside memorably said to her husband, "You go on and enjoy yourself, and I'll join you in a little while". The next day he briefly brightened enough to give her a kiss; then died, confident that his beloved would join him soon. Whether in a hospital bed or under a steamroller, Christians can die fully confident of eternal joy in God's presence.

For, by union with the Son of God by faith, all believers are adopted into God's family as his firstborn sons, entitled to a glorious inheritance in the resurrected creation, the kingdom of heaven. All that Christians need do to receive this inheritance is... die. Even I can manage that!

This hope of a heavenly inheritance was clearly a healthy corrective for these Ephesian elders, living in a wealthy and cosmopolitan city where their contemporaries lived largely to indulge themselves and hoard up material things for their children. Our inheritance in heaven frees us from slavery to the acquisition of worldly comforts for sacrificial service.

Our inheritance is also important evangelistically. Peter writes:

> "Always be prepared to give an answer to everyone who asks you to give the reason for the hope that you have."
>
> 1 Peter 3:15

For beneath the veneer of confidence that money buys, and especially as we become frail or discover a cancer, many unbelievers are rightly afraid of what lies beyond the grave. Our culture says, "Eat, drink and be merry for tomorrow we die"—but when the party's over, and we collect up the empty wine bottles, the fear still gnaws away at our souls. Our world offers tons of misguided faith and gallons of temporary love—but solid resurrection hope? That is a rare treasure!

Moreover, heaven is the comfort we need when we grieve

for loved ones who died trusting Christ or when we face death ourselves, whether we are lying down in front of a steamroller or fighting for breath in a hospital bed.

In Revelation 22, God has sent us a stunning snapshot of the resurrected creation inheritance awaiting us, full of stunning Old Testament symbolism to encourage us:

> "Then the angel showed me **the river of the water of life**, as clear as crystal, flowing from the throne of God and of the Lamb down the middle of the great street of the city. On each side of the river stood **the tree of life**, bearing twelve crops of fruit, yielding its fruit every month. And the leaves of the tree are for the healing of the nations. No longer will there be any curse. **The throne of God and of the Lamb** will be in the city, and **his servants** will serve him. They will see his face, and his name will be on their foreheads. There will be no more night. They will not need the light of a lamp or the light of the sun, for the Lord God will give them light. And they will reign for ever and ever." Revelation 22:1-5 (bold text mine)

Here, at the end of Revelation and the Bible, we're given a glimpse of a garden-city paradise, where God's people have been rescued and regenerated by the death and resurrection of Jesus.

This heavenly city of Jerusalem includes not just updated features from the Garden of Eden, but the civilisation of kings and nations, purified and intensified. It is God's "extreme makeover" of the cosmos as a wedding gift for his Son and a home for his people. Let me briefly show you around your new home...

The river: spiritual abundance (Rev 22:1)

The river of the water of life is depicted as watering this whole garden city with an inexhaustible torrent of life-giving water. It will be "clear as crystal" to keep us spiritually clean. Its course is "down the middle of the great street", recalling the promise of a highway of holiness (Isaiah 35:8), where the redeemed will walk at leisure along this beautiful boulevard, soaking up the happy atmosphere. But this river is far greater than the Amazon or the Nile, because it's far more than H2O...

God promised in Ezekiel 47 that a flood of blessing would one day flow from his presence. In that vision, Ezekiel walked into this stream, ankle-deep at first, soon knee-deep, and then waist-deep, and finally into an ocean of blessing to bathe in. Jesus announced to a Samaritan woman drawing water from a well, "Whoever drinks the water I give them will never thirst. Indeed, the water I give them will become in them a spring of water welling up to eternal life" (John 4:14). He later explained:

> "'Let anyone who is thirsty come to me and drink.
> Whoever believes in me, as Scripture has said, rivers of
> living water will flow from within them.' By this he meant
> the Spirit."   John 7:37-39

Now, in Revelation, we again hear his gracious invitation, "Come! Let the one who is thirsty come ... take the free gift of the water of life" (Revelation 22:17). This means that although Jesus seals us with his Spirit when first we believe in him, as "a deposit guaranteeing our inheritance" (Ephesians 1:14), this is only the first course of the feast to come in heaven. We will never be entirely filled or satisfied in this world—indeed, we will often feel spiritually dry. But one day in heaven, Jesus will provide this torrent of thirst-quenching satisfaction and life-giving cleansing by filling us with his Holy Spirit.

So if you're thirsty for eternal life, come to Jesus and enjoy your first drink of life from his Holy Spirit—and then look forward to being completely filled, satisfied, cleansed and refreshed by the Spirit of the living God in heaven... from the river of the water of life!

The tree: permanent deliverance (Rev 22:2)

On each side of the river stood "the tree of life". This tree was originally sustaining Adam and Eve in the Garden of Eden. When they rebelled and were denied access to this tree, they were effectively condemned to death.

However, again in Ezekiel 47, God promised not just one tree but an orchard of nourishment: "Fruit trees of all kinds will grow on both banks of the river" (v 12). This escalation of blessing is found here in Revelation with a tree growing over both sides of the river, "bearing twelve crops of fruit", symbolising complete nourishment for all God's people. The leaves of the tree "are for the healing of the nations", permanently healing the damage of sin in our souls and decay in our bodies.

It's thrilling to discover that the word for "tree" here is not the usual word, but a word meaning "wood". Three times in Acts, Peter used this word, condemning those who killed Jesus by "hanging him on a wood" (5:30; 10:39; 13:29); and he later writes of Jesus, "'He himself bore our sins' in his body on the *wood* ... 'by his wounds you have been healed'" (1 Peter 2:24).

So the tree or "wood" of life symbolises the cross on which Jesus died for our sin, removing from us for ever the curse of God's judgment! The tree of life in the original Garden of Eden was a living symbol of the future cross of Christ; the tree of life in this new creation is a living symbol recalling the cross of Christ. In this world, we shall never be entirely free from the damage of our sin in our characters and our relationships. But one day, in heaven, our permanent deliverance from God's judgment and eternal healing from the damage of sin will for ever derive from the death of Jesus, who was nailed to the wooden timbers of a Roman cross. The "tree of life" represents the cross.

The servants: privileged presence (Rev 22:3-5)

We will serve him. The word implies the service of high priests in the temple. For we shall all have access to worship him perfectly with all of our life in heaven. What a joy it will be to please our Father with perfect obedience rather than constantly failing him.

We will see his face. Have you ever wondered what Jesus' face looks like? Or how wonderful it will be when he calls us forward by name to meet him? To feel—as we fall flat on our faces before him and mumble our anxious apologies— his pierced hands on our shoulders, lifting us up to find him smiling. To hear his promised words of genuine approval: "Well done, good and faithful servant ... Come and share your master's happiness!" (Matthew 25:21). The exact tone of his words and that smile on his face will be thrilling for eternity and make every hardship here worthwhile.

We will have his name on our foreheads. We will openly belong to him. I've always wanted an impressive tattoo like David Beckham. And as we walk around heaven, angels will see God's family name written on us and make way for the honoured children of God. His name means we will publicly belong to him—like a bride with a new surname—entitling us to the privileges of God's family!

We will reign for ever. What a paradox of grace that pardoned slaves will reign with the king of heaven. We have foolishly squandered and selfishly exploited the resources of this planet. But the Lamb will lead us to govern the new creation with wisdom and selfless integrity.

Can you grasp how epically wonderful it will be to be there in the presence of God? I won't bore you with the whole story, but on August 4th 2012, at the London Olympic Games, I was fortunate to be in the Olympic stadium with three of my children when Jessica Ennis, Greg Rutherford and Mo Farah each won gold medals in 46 glorious minutes. The joy was uncontained, the noise was insane, the experience more fabulous than anything I've ever experienced in sport. But I whispered to my daughter at the end, "If this is what it's like for some athletes who can jump far, throw a spear and run a long way, how good will it be when the King of kings comes on stage?" It will be INSANELY FABULOUS to be there!

Knowing Jesus makes everything in life better—but don't be too disappointed when life in this world isn't perfect. We must struggle and suffer in a world under judgment as we take up our cross to follow Jesus. But one day we'll realise, to quote the classic Bachman-Turner Overdrive song again, "Baby, you ain't seen nothin' yet"!

This hope of heaven stimulates our evangelism

This description of the heavenly paradise with its river, tree, throne and servants is a motive for mission, because we long for our family, friends and colleagues to be with us in paradise rather than in the eternal, conscious torment of hell. It's also part of the message we proclaim. If we only talk about life as Christians now, many will find it hard to see why it's worth becoming a Christian. But if we talk of the future, the difference between the happiness of heaven and the horror of hell is obvious, and the need of our Saviour is clear.

This hope of heaven sustains our faith

We will certainly not be disappointed when we get there. We'll find that God is unceasingly marvellous—indeed, our most satisfying joy. In his book *Heaven*, J.C. Ryle wrote movingly of how believers should think about eternity:

> *"Let us not be afraid to meditate often on the subject of heaven, and to rejoice in the prospect of good things to come. I know that even a believer's heart will sometimes fail when he thinks of the last enemy which is death and the unseen world beyond. Jordan (death) is a cold river to cross at best, and not a few tremble when they think of their own crossing. But let us take comfort in the remembrance of the other side. Think, Christian believer, of seeing your Saviour, and beholding your King in his beauty. Faith will at last be swallowed up in sight and hope in certainty. Think of the many loved ones gone before you, and of the happy meeting between you and them. You are not going to a foreign country; you are going home. You are not going to dwell amongst strangers, but among friends. You will find them all safe, all well, all ready to greet you, all prepared to join in one unbroken song of praise. Then let us take comfort and persevere. With such prospects before us, we may well cry, 'It is worthwhile being a Christian'."*

Think it through

1. What do you most look forward to about the new creation?

2. How can the hope of heaven sustain us in times of difficulty and suffering?

3. How should the hope of heaven affect our evangelism?

Church leaders: *How can you ensure that the future judgment, heaven and hell, and the consequent need of our Saviour are appropriately taught in your church?*

20. Help the weak

because it's more blessed to give than to receive

*"I have not coveted anyone's silver or gold or clothing. You
yourselves know that these hands of mine have supplied my
own needs and the needs of my companions. In everything
I did, I showed you that by this kind of hard work we must
help the weak, remembering the words the Lord Jesus
himself said: 'It is more blessed to give than to receive.'"*

Acts 20:33-35

With echoes of a speech by Samuel the prophet (1 Samuel
12), Paul reminds the Ephesians of his financial integrity and
sacrificial generosity. In particular, he was commending his
labours in raising financial support for himself and his team
in gospel ministry. But he clearly saw this as an example of
two broader principles: namely, that "we must help the weak",
and, as Jesus said, "It is more blessed to give than to receive".
These principles raise issues that are much discussed among
Reformed churches: these centre on the place of welfare
ministries and social justice issues in the life of our churches.

Are social ministries a distraction?

Different churches offer different approaches...

Some churches probably wouldn't encourage their members to get involved in social initiatives at all, in case they'll be distracted from evangelism—even if they aren't actually doing much of either. I've noticed, however, that although all our church plants have been focused upon evangelistic outreach, as they've grown, they've attracted new church members with skills and opportunities to be active in a range of social ministries which also provide opportunities to speak about Christ, such as our crisis pregnancy ministry, prison visiting, debt counselling, outreach to the homeless, biblical counselling, street pastoring, and so on. Should we encourage or discourage such involvement?

Other churches approve of these ministries for individuals but not for churches. They rightly observe that too much involvement in social justice has often led churches away from the gospel. They suggest that social justice should be left to para-church ministries and individuals, while churches should concentrate on Word ministries. Is that right?

Other churches still would encourage their members to get involved in social-welfare ministry of every kind and, whether or not there is any gospel conversation, call it mission. At the Lausanne Congress for World Evangelisation in Cape Town, there was this same emphasis upon the need for justice and the alleviation of suffering. Many Reformed evangelicals welcomed the timely intervention of John Piper at that event, urging us to remember that...

"In all the attempts to alleviate suffering, we must not forget to alleviate eternal suffering by the proclamation of Christ."

This rightly prioritises evangelism. But does that mean that church members shouldn't get involved in social justice at all?

Let's briefly explore what the Bible says...

God is clearly concerned for the poor

The Bible repeatedly celebrates our Creator's concern for our whole being, in both our physical and spiritual needs; for example, "I am the LORD, who exercises kindness, justice and righteousness on earth, for in these I delight" (Jeremiah 9:24). The needy are repeatedly described in four categories: *orphans* (surely including children aborted or neglected in government institutions), *widows* (surely including women abused and trafficked in our cities), *foreigners* (surely including the asylum seekers at our borders and the homeless on our streets), and *the poor* (surely including many single parents, elderly, disabled and long-term unemployed struggling to make ends meet).

Where these obligations were once laid upon the nation of Israel, it is now appropriate for churches to accept such concerns for their own members.

Ensure that the church are cared for—but don't distract the Bible-teachers

James warns:

> "Suppose a brother or a sister is without clothes and daily food. If one of you says to them, 'Go in peace; keep warm and well-fed,' but does nothing about their physical needs, what good is it? In the same way, faith by itself, if it is not accompanied by action, is dead."
>
> James 2:15-17

However, when faced with a serious neglect of Greek-speaking widows in the church famine-relief programme, the Apostles refused to be distracted from their teaching ministries, declaring, "It would not be right for us to neglect the ministry of the word" (Acts 6:2). But they didn't close their eyes to the needy in the church; they organised the recruitment of godly and wise people to be commissioned with delegated responsibility and supported in prayer, to manage the relief programme; so they clarified the priority of Word ministry but ensured the provision of relief ministry. When we read of the impact of this approach—"so the word of God spread" (Acts 6:7)—we need to remember that *two* things happened in Jerusalem: the teachers prepared excellent sermons *and* an excellent team was appointed to feed the hungry in the church.

Love your neighbour—like the Good Samaritan

What about unbelievers—outside the church? Can we dismiss the social needs of unbelievers in our community, when Jesus challenged his disciples to sell their possessions, give radically and get involved in the lives of the poor, saying, "When you give a banquet, invite the poor, the crippled, the lame, the blind" (Luke 14:13)? In Luke 4, Jesus declares that the Old Testament promise of an evangelist announcing good news to the poor (Isaiah 61) is fulfilled in their hearing— indicating that his synagogue audience were the poor in view, meaning spiritually poor and in need of the gospel. But Jesus' famous parable of the Good Samaritan (Luke 10) is plainly about helping those we come across in physical need—it really would be bizarre to interpret this parable as solely concerned with evangelism. This is especially so when we recognise that Jesus, having prayerfully concluded that his priority was preaching the gospel and not healing (Mark 1:38), continues to heal those who come to him in need! Clearly, while he did not organise social reform, Jesus did not ignore those he met in physical need as he went about preaching the gospel! So how can churches maintain Jesus' priority of Word ministry while obeying Jesus' teaching in the parable of the Good Samaritan?

In our mission to an unbelieving world: "especially" clarifies an emphasis

Christians can't do evangelism only, because God's Word requires more of us. But we also can't do everything with equal urgency, and our resources are limited. Jesus and his Apostles practised the *priority* of gospel ministry (Mark 1:38; Acts 6:4). However, the word *priority* is sometimes heard as being dispassionately exclusive, meaning *nothing but evangelism*. So it may be more helpful to use Paul's word, *"especially"*—"Let us do good to all people, especially to those who belong to the family of believers" (Galatians 6:10), implying that our church family is a priority, but we should still be a blessing to our community.

Social justice and evangelism are both ways of loving our neighbours. The first has great but temporary benefits for this world, while the second has glorious benefits both now and in the world to come. So, in understanding how they relate, we have found three enormously helpful principles that are illustrated in Jesus' parable of the Good Samaritan. These will need to be applied differently in different contexts:

a) Especially the needy (read Luke 10:30)

Jesus pictures a man being mugged on the notoriously dangerous road from Jerusalem to Jericho: "… attacked by robbers. They stripped him of his clothes, beat him and went away, leaving him half-dead." We might have said, "They bashed him over the head with a baseball bat, stabbed him in the back with a beer bottle and kicked him to the ground, took his phone, wallet and trainers, and left him unconscious in a pool of blood."

Jesus describes something that could happen to any of us. We could be mugged by thieves or by redundancy, by a cancerous lump or the death of a child, by a creeping addiction to gambling or to pornography. Many of us already have been. We could self-righteously enquire what this man was doing travelling alone. But Jesus doesn't bother with blame. We all make bad decisions and do stupid things. It's ugly when the well and wealthy criticise the poor and sick because of contributory foolishness; and it's particularly ugly in Christians, for Christ saved us despite the stupidity of our own sin. Jesus is plainly telling us to be concerned for those in need.

There has sometimes been among Reformed evangelicals an accepted strategy of concentrating upon the elite of our society in the name of strategically accessing leadership potential—while little effort is made to reach more ordinary communities. Apart from the fact that many great leaders come from challenging backgrounds, we do need to reach privileged school kids, students and young professionals. But they then need to be deployed to gradually reach all the communities of our cities, and not just to replenish churches and ministries that reach the elites and ignore the poor. And then we need the resource-rich congregations to support churches that are reaching resource-poor communities.

2. Especially our neighbours (read Luke 10:31–32)
God commands us to love our neighbours as generously as we love ourselves. Jesus was not limiting those we help to those who are closest to us; rather, Jesus was expanding our definition of neighbours to include anyone we come across in need, whatever their race, religion, class or kind of problem!

In Jesus' story, the priests and the Levites who passed by were respected leaders of the community who distributed temple money for poor Jews. How would we react if we came across a man slumped in a gutter, covered in blood, outside a remote train station? You can imagine their thoughts...

- *I don't know him—he could be dangerous or drag me into endless problems or even sue me—and the thugs might be just round the corner!*
- *I'm already late for an important meeting, and I'll let people down, including my family!*
- *I do many good things for God—and there'll always be poor people. I must keep my evangelistic priority and courageously pass by!*

Jesus was highlighting the selfishness of mankind, found even in the best of us, but particularly the religious version that devalues practical love. Jesus wasn't suggesting that the priest and Levite should abandon their church ministries to search the roads of Palestine for battered travellers (and the Samaritan went on with his life after caring for the injured man) And Jesus wasn't telling us to help everyone, for we all feel bewildered by the scale of need even in our own neighbourhood, let alone the world. He's telling us to help *the one person we can all help*—the needy person we come across in daily life.

Jesus doesn't for a minute suggest anyone should abandon gospel work for social justice. But none of us are doing gospel work all the time. Jesus wasn't telling churches to divert resources from gospel preaching into poverty relief. He was telling individual disciples to put ourselves out for someone in need. We can each help one elderly lady in our block of flats, one distressed colleague at work, or one migrant family in our area trying to find work. For we were all lying in the spiritual gutter when Jesus found us. And...

3. Especially with the gospel (read Luke 10:33-35)

We'll want to meet *any* need, but *especially* people's need of the gospel.

Jesus describes the compassion of the Samaritan in these words: "Then he put the man on his own donkey, brought him to an inn and took care of him The next day he took out two denarii and gave them to the innkeeper." So, rather than abandon the man as soon as possible, or just call an ambulance, he drove him to the hospital and covered the costs.

This was practical love—involving costly self-denial. Samaritans were generally hated by the Jews. But this Samaritan didn't allow his own experience of prejudice to become an excuse to neglect a foreigner in need. He didn't harden his heart with scorn or with a social strategy for discouraging dependency. He didn't offer help in order to earn favour with God, nor in the hope that the wounded man would be grateful and join his church! He just did it for the man's sake, out of compassion; he "took pity on him".

But when we think of how Christ offered his sacrificial practical love for us, we realise that the greatest Samaritan love is evangelism. For everyone's most desperate need is for the Saviour (indeed, the most potent force for social change is evangelism, because only God's Spirit working through God's Word can bring someone to repent of social evil and transform human hearts). Christ is the "Great Samaritan", who came to us in our desperate spiritual need and rescued us from dying in the gutter of sin.

When we get involved in compassionate care, we shouldn't do so just to gain evangelistic opportunities. This can easily become manipulative subterfuge. We should offer our works of compassion as simply the justice and righteousness in which God delights. But opportunities often do arise when people wonder why we help them, and *the gospel is the most precious gift we can offer*—for evangelism is compassionate care to relieve eternal suffering.

Indeed, evangelism is the most loving mercy ministry there is.

And when we're not busy with evangelism, let's welcome opportunities to help a needy neighbour—because Jesus says bluntly in verse 37, "Go and do likewise"!

In summary then, there are different roles given to churches and members. Our churches and their leaders should be focused upon equipping believers for their ministries of making disciples of all nations, in the church and in the world. So church pastors must ensure that the needy in the church are being properly cared for... *but not by them*. They must devote themselves to prayer and the ministry of the Word, which equips the believers for their ministries, including being like the Good Samaritan.

As individual believers, we will seek to live and work in a distinctively compassionate way. We may be able to choose jobs with a significant social impact, or with political influence, or high-earning careers that will generate funding for reaching the needy, especially with gospel ministry.

Indeed, sacrificial fundraising for gospel ministry is the particular example of helping the weak that Paul commends to these Elders. Christian workers often don't have opportunities or skills to raise the financial support they need. Becoming a patron of gospel ministries, at whatever level we can, is a most dignified heritage, which can be traced back not only to big supporters like Monmouth, Thornton and the Countess of Huntingdon (financing the gospel work of William Tyndale, John Newton and Charles Simeon respectively) but to the Apostle Paul himself (with a menial and back-breaking job in leather "tent-making"). In all of life, we are to live compassionately like the good Samaritan... *especially* towards the needy, *especially* towards our neighbours, and *especially* with the gospel... pointing people to the Greatest Samaritan of all—to Jesus.

Think it through

1. *It's easy to feel overwhelmed by the physical needs of the world. How can the parable of the Good Samaritan help us do something?*

2. *How is what Jesus wants from his churches different to what he wants from individual believers?*

3. *How can we make evangelism our primary mercy ministry?*

Church leaders: *How can your church preserve the priority of Word ministry for making disciples, while encouraging all members to be good Samaritans like Jesus?*

21. Pray with confidence

because God is our heavenly Father

"When Paul had finished speaking, he knelt down with all of them and prayed." Acts 20:36

It was clearly the most natural thing for Paul and his friends to kneel in prayer as they said farewell. For prayer just means speaking to God. He speaks to us through the words of the Bible and we respond to him in the words of prayer. Prayer is like breathing—if it gets restricted, we become ill.

Most Western churches have much to learn from other Christian cultures. I'll never forget coming into our church building to take part in a Korean-congregation event to find 400 Koreans on their knees, crying out to God in prayer all at the same time, many in tears. I asked my Korean colleague, "What are they praying about so passionately?" He replied, "They're crying out to God for this country!" That was humbling.

But what is prayer?

In his classic little book, *Praying in the Spirit* (published in 1662), written from Bedford Jail, John Bunyan—author of *A Pilgrim's Progress*— brilliantly defined prayer as:

> *"A sincere, sensible, affectionate pouring out of the heart or soul to God, through Christ, in the strength and assistance of the Spirit, for such things as God has promised, or according to his Word, for the good of the church, with submission in faith to the will of God."*

Bunyan wanted prayer to be genuine and not just empty waffle that our Father will ignore:

- **Real prayer is "sincere"** (honest and genuine), for otherwise, "when you ask, you do not receive, because you ask with wrong motives" (James 4:3).

- **Real prayer is "sensible"** (fervent and passionate), because "you will seek me and find me when you seek me with all your heart" (Jeremiah 29:13).

- **Real prayer is "affectionate"** (confident in God's goodness), for "the one who doubts is like a wave of the sea, blown and tossed by the wind. That person should not expect to receive anything from the Lord" (James 1:6).

- **Real prayer is "through Christ, in the strength and assistance of the Spirit"** (empowered and conveyed to the Father by the Holy Spirit), for "the Spirit himself intercedes for us through wordless groans" (Romans 8:26).

- **Real prayer is "for such things as God has promised"** (claiming what God has offered in his Word), for "this is the confidence we have in approaching God: that if we ask anything according to his will, he hears us" (1 John 5:14).

- **Real prayer is "for the good of the church"** (not selfish, but for all God's people), for we must "keep on praying for all the Lord's people" (Ephesians 6:18).

- **Real prayer is "with submission in faith to the will of God"** (surrendering to God's will rather than asserting our own), for "how much more will your Father in heaven give good gifts to those who ask him" (Matthew 7:11).

Bunyan understood that God answers the genuine prayers of his children.

But how should we pray?

Jesus teaches us how to pray in the "Lord's Prayer" (Matthew 6:9-13). It's perfect because:

It comes from the Lord of prayer

Jesus is the prayer expert. As God, he knows what sort of prayer God will answer; as God's Son, he knows how to approach the Father; as a man, he understands our weakness. In addition to daily Jewish prayers, the Gospels emphasise Jesus' private devotions and response to crises: "Jesus often withdrew to lonely places and prayed" (Luke 5:16). Indeed, as our mediator and older brother, he's praying for us now in the presence of our Father. In the Lord's Prayer, we're learning from the Lord of Prayer.

It is a wonderfully flexible prayer

In Luke 11, Jesus gives the prayer as words to use (though not to repeat mindlessly), and in Matthew 6, as a pattern to be expanded in all our prayers. Since Jesus was speaking before his death and resurrection, he left some phrases undeveloped. We can enlarge each with later teaching and personal application, for the Lord's Prayer is simple enough for kids but deep enough for scholars.

It gives a gospel shape to prayer

The Lord's Prayer is a work of divine genius and a miracle of theological compression.

A few simple words reveal the impact of the gospel upon us: in Christ, God is our *Father* (the opening address), our *Lord* (the first three petitions) and our *Saviour* (the second three petitions). It reveals Christ's priorities for prayer and life—and such prayer is part of the disciplined righteousness required by Jesus in his "Sermon on the Mount", which is all about living for our heavenly Father (Matthew 5 – 7).

Indeed, the Lord's Prayer seems upside down to sinners. The first requests concern God—"your name", "your kingdom" and "your will". Only then do we ask for the *provision, pardon* and *protection* we need. This is because genuine Christian prayer isn't about getting God to surrender to us, like some genie in a bottle ready to obey us. Prayer is about surrendering ourselves to God's plans and priorities.

This is a gospel-shaped prayer for private devotions, visiting someone in hospital, around the family table or in church. It's also a great summary of Christian doctrine for teaching to believers and explaining to unbelievers. Although our Father may patiently tolerate endless silly requests, like loving parents tolerating a toddler constantly demanding sweets, this prayer is the kind of prayer that God really delights to answer.

Pray to Our Father in heaven (Matthew 6:9)

We forget how stunning it is to call our Creator and Ruler "our Father". The Aramaic *Abba* means "Dad" (affectionate but respectful). No human religion or Jewish teacher ever dared to call the living God "Dad".

Jesus knew that the first principle and rocket engine that drives us to pray is not *technique* but *theology*—not *how* we pray but *who* we pray to. His opening summarises the entire gospel work of Christ, the miracle of grace and the basis of prayer. By faith in Christ, believers are "incorporated" into him, so we share in his privileges. So prayer begins, "Our Father in heaven". We say "our" aware of the needs of others, "in heaven" respectfully and confidently, aware that he is the Almighty who dwells on high, and "Father", aware that he loves us passionately.

Unlike human fathers, he's always available, always knows what's best, and is always patient and kind, always able to do what's necessary. He's generous but wise, firm but forgiving, ever faithful to us and always with us—the best father anyone could want. Here we might especially thank God for Jesus, in whom we enjoy these privileges.

In the petitions, we submit to our Father as Lord and Saviour.

Pray to the Father as our Lord (Matthew 6:9-10)

The first three petitions commit us to his glory, kingdom and will:

- **Hallowed be your name**, meaning "may your character be glorified and honoured by all". God's names reveal his character; so *El Elyon* means "God most high"; *Yahweh* (LORD) means "faithful Redeemer"; and *Jesus* means "God saves". At this name all people, presidents and prophets will one day bow. To "hallow" is to honour with reverent speech and behaviour this God revealed in Jesus. Here we might express our personal adoration of God.

- **Your kingdom come**, meaning "may your rule be welcomed everywhere". Christ's kingdom is being established by gospel preaching in the hearts of those who submit to Christ, but it is not of this world and will come with Christ. Here we submit to Christ, ask for others to come to Christ, and long for Christ to return and end this world. Here we might ask for our friends to be converted.

- **Your will be done**, meaning "may your plans be accomplished in everything". God's will is both what he decrees will happen all around us, and also what he commands in the Bible should happen within us. This request implies our surrender to God's plans for ourselves and our world. Here we might ask for his will to be done in the particular activities and business of the day.

Pray to the Father as our Saviour (Matthew 6:11-13)

The second three petitions rely on our Father for all that we really need:

- **Give us today our daily bread** *(Provision)*: We recognise that we and others depend upon God daily. Alluding to the "manna" provided from heaven for Israel, "daily bread" includes our physical needs for food, clothing, jobs and homes; our spiritual need for the "living bread" of Christ; and our eternal need of life in the Sabbath rest of his kingdom. Indeed, we are asking God to sustain us in everything with his "bread", who is Jesus. Here we might ask our Father for all our particular personal and church needs.

- **Forgive us our debts** *(Pardon)*: We confess our sins, ask for forgiveness and renew our repentance. We confess and apologise, not because our pardon is now in doubt but to restore our relationship with our Father. We renew our commitment to forgive others and we pray for enemies (for only those impacted by forgiveness enough to forgive others may assume they are forgiven). Here we might confess our particular sins and thank him that we are forgiven because of Jesus dying and living for us.

- **Deliver us from evil** *(Protection):* We ask for protection from the testing of suffering and the temptation of Satan. Since Satan has been defeated at the cross but is not yet destroyed, we ask for continuing deliverance from him through Christ, who has conquered him. Here we might ask for deliverance from the particular lies afflicting our family or church.

Jesus is teaching us that the first principle of prayer is to know who we're talking to: the Father who loves us, the LORD who rules us, and the Saviour who cares for us!

But why do we need to pray?

If prayer is not about getting God to submit to our wills, but about submitting ourselves to his will, the obvious next question is why we bother to pray? If God "does not lie or *change his mind*" (1 Samuel 15:29), and if he "knows what you need *before* you ask him" (Matthew 6:8), then what is the point of praying at all?

The great Reformer John Calvin clarified six biblical reasons for prayer:

1. To depend upon him
2. To purify the desires of our hearts
3. To be content with whatever our Father provides
4. To appreciate more deeply God's generosity and faithfulness to us

5. To enjoy without guilt his many gifts

6. To trust God to provide our daily needs and never let us down

Calvin summarised such prayer as "digging up the treasures" promised in Scripture. It's our experience that God delays giving us the things he plans to give us until we ask for them in prayer. Though God has always planned to give them, he encourages us in prayer by withholding them until we ask. So things happen when we pray!

So let's pray...

Think it through

1. *Why do we so often struggle with prayer? What truths in this chapter help address this?*

2. *What is so special about the Lord's Prayer—how could we make more use of it? Why not ask someone who seems to have a fulfilling prayer life about their motivations and methods of prayer.*

3. *Spend some time praying—perhaps praying the Lord's prayer in Matthew 6:9-13 phrase by phrase. In particular, respond to Acts 20 by praying that you and your family and church would be shaped by the priorities of Paul here.*

Church leaders: *How can you ensure that you are praying appropriately for your church?*

22. Keep going to all nations

to make disciples for Christ

"What grieved them most was his statement that they
would never see his face again. Then they accompanied him
to the ship." Acts 20:38

Why not stay in Ephesus—or at least return there after taking
the financial gift from the Greek churches to Jerusalem?

Strategically, it was ideal. Ephesus was the cosmopolitan
regional capital of Galatia, right at the heart of the Roman
Empire. Paul could help the Ephesian church develop its
flagship role in leading, resourcing and extending the network
of churches that Paul had planted over recent years (like the
seven named in Revelation 2 – 3). These churches were far from
firmly established—false teaching and persecution abounded.
He clearly now had this encouraging group of receptive Elders
to work with—and most church ministries benefit from godly
and gifted leaders staying a long time. Wasn't it irresponsible for
him to leave the Ephesian church to such inexperienced Elders
when the ministry was still fragile but so full of potential?

And for Paul, personally, it was surely advisable to settle down, at least for a while. The toll on his health of constant beatings and imprisonments (v 23, see 2 Corinthians 11) must have been severe. All things considered, it must have seemed like madness for Paul to announce that he was leaving and would never see these leaders again! We know from Romans 15:23-25 that he planned to travel to Jerusalem, on to Rome and then to Spain to open a new field of mission. What was his problem? Was he afflicted with an absurdly restless spirit, or some kind of death-wish, or worse—ambition for his own glory?

Why did Paul so relentlessly pursue evangelism, church-planting and cross-cultural mission? The answer is important for all of us in charting the course of our lives, but perhaps especially for parents and churches wondering if they should encourage more of their godly and gifted young people to offer themselves for training in these gospel ministries full-time.

The best explanation for Paul's incessant missionary enterprise is simply that he was doing everything he could to accomplish the task for which the risen Jesus had saved him on the road to Damascus: "This man is my chosen instrument to proclaim my name to the Gentiles [or 'nations']" (Acts 9:15). In fact, Paul was leading in the same mission to which the risen Jesus has called all of us in his "Great Commission", widely recognised as his mission statement for all believers, individually and collectively:

> "**All** authority in heaven and on earth has been given
> to me. Therefore go and **make disciples of *all* nations**,
> baptising them in the name of the Father and of the
> Son and of the Holy Spirit, and teaching them to obey
> *everything* I have commanded you. And surely I am
> with you *always*, to the very end of the age."
>
> Matthew 28:18-20 (bold text and italics mine)

The four great "alls" of Jesus' words here have enormous implications for making disciples of all nations through evangelism, church-planting and cross-cultural mission today.

1. "All authority" means we must try to reach EVERYWHERE.
2. "All nations" means we try to tell EVERYONE.
3. "Everything [or 'all'] I have commanded you" means we try to teach EVERYTHING.
4. "Always" means we try to take EVERY OPPORTUNITY.

"All authority" means we try to reach EVERYWHERE

Our reason for making disciples is that Christ is risen and enthroned on high with absolute and eternal supremacy over heaven and earth; that is, everywhere! As Her Majesty the Queen addresses the UK Parliament each year to publish the reform programme of her government, here Jesus outlines his plans for his world for all time. This little speech has impacted our planet more than any other, including, "We will fight them on the beaches", "I have a dream" and "Yes, we can"! For this "Great Commission" launched the gospel movement which is still transforming our planet today.

His claim to all authority has three implications:

- **Everywhere belongs to Jesus:** There are no nations or cities that don't belong to Jesus. Africa can claim to be Muslim, China can claim to be Communist, and Britain can claim to be secular, but in truth, they all belong to Jesus. So every district and every street of every village, town and city belongs to Jesus and is accountable to his judgment.

- **Everywhere must be reached for Jesus:** This commission is not a suggestion or invitation but the command of the risen Jesus. Though the penalty for disobedience has been suffered by Jesus, we'll be judged or rewarded in eternity by our commitment or neglect of this command.

- **Everywhere can be reached for Jesus:** Because Jesus rules everywhere. Even if he permits us the honour of facing opposition or more serious persecution, Jesus is in charge: more protective than any police force, more influential than any government, with more resources than any bank. We can attempt to reach the unreached of the most inhospitable Amazonian-jungle tribes, or the most hostile urban-jungle gangs, because Jesus even rules there.

So in every parish, village, town and city in every nation, we need to do what we can to evangelise churches into existence: among children and young people in the suburbs and in the deprived tower blocks, among students in universities and young workers in their plush offices, in ethnic communities and in elderly care homes—and irrespective of possessive opposition from denominational, religious or secular authorities. "All authority" means we must try to reach everywhere!

"All nations" means we must try to tell EVERYONE

It was a shock for me to realise that making disciples of all nations is not just a command for some people with a bizarre interest in people of strange cultures. God has always planned to give to his Son a beautiful bride of people from every tribe and tongue, saved by his death on a cross. God's creation mandate for mankind to fill the earth and subdue it (Genesis 1:28) is fulfilled through global evangelism; God's promise to Abraham to bless all nations (Genesis 12:3) is fulfilled through international mission; God's call to his Servant to be his light to all nations (Isaiah 42:6; 49:6) is fulfilled through cross-cultural church-planting. As someone once put it, we're all "knots in the net that Jesus has thrown over his world".

The word "go" (literally, "going") has the sense of "as we go" through each day, rather than going abroad. But the word still has a sense of movement. Following our cross-cultural missionary, evangelist and church-planting Lord, we will have to leave our comfort zone to make disciples. We will need to learn how to welcome internationals who visit our cities for business, education and tourism; we will need to learn how to plant churches among ethnic and social communities of every kind; we need to learn how to recruit and send people and maintain support for international mission agencies of every kind and to faithfully pray for them; and we will need to learn how to welcome opportunities to partner with foreign missionaries coming to our cities.

"All that I've commanded" means we must try to teach EVERYTHING

Baptising new believers into the trinitarian name of God, we're to teach them not part but all of Jesus' teaching in all the Bible. There are three implications:

- We need to ensure that gifted and trained **Bible-teachers are involved** in leading our evangelism, planting and cross-cultural ministries, and not expect our initiatives to thrive under leaders with inadequate learning or who lack the necessary gifts.

- We mustn't burden our evangelistic teams, church-plants and missions with **unrealistic expectations of**

speedy numerical growth—for the deep work of the Spirit through the Word will need time, especially in hardened cultures.

- We mustn't deploy evangelists, plant churches or establish missions with shallow-rooted, diseased or tangled plants. If we deploy shallow plants (immature evangelists), they will give up when it gets costly; if we plant with diseased plants (unsound planting teams), they will soon experience division and conflict; if we establish tangled plants (missions distracted by secular priorities), we'll soon have missions exhausted and resentful because there is no spiritual fruit.

If Jesus commands us to make disciples by teaching his Word, we need to initiate evangelism, church-planting and cross-cultural mission with people well-trained and appropriately gifted in God's Word, such as these Ephesian Elders being taught by Paul!

"Always" means we must try to take EVERY OPPORTUNITY

"And surely I am with you always" is the wonderful assurance of the presence and power of the Spirit of Christ whenever we're making disciples of all nations for him. We're never alone and never abandoned. Indeed, he's not joining our mission—we're joining his; and the greatest joy of evangelism, planting churches and cross-cultural mission is watching him powerfully at work. If you want to get know Jesus well, throw yourself into making disciples of all nations for him. There are three implications:

- **Weariness need not stop us:** God's power is made perfect in weakness and we must keep going, for studies show that continuing momentum is crucial for establishing thriving missions and church-planting movements.

- **Risks need not stop us:** There are no guarantees of success and there is always a risk that something might not work (in the generally exciting story of God growing our movement, we have painfully had to close two of our most faithful church plants); but anything obedient is possible, and when we are obedient anything is possible, because God is involved. So the extraordinary growth of the gospel in South Korea accelerated when the pages of the Bible of a Welsh missionary, Robert Thomas, beheaded in 1865, were used to wallpaper a man's house. The man started reading his "wallpaper" and was converted, as were other visitors, until a church was formed. Today 30% of South Koreans profess to be Reformed evangelical Christians!

- **Costs need not stop us:** Often it isn't the costs of mission to our own comfort and wellbeing, but the costs we perceive may fall upon our families and friends that discourage us from volunteering for evangelism, church-planting and cross-cultural mission. But apart from allowing them the privilege of accepting costs in serving Christ, we can trust almighty God to provide for them too. It's often not realised by those who quote the decisive moment in Hudson Taylor's decision to become a missionary to China on the beach at Brighton, England, that the last hurdle was not fear for himself but for those who would got to China with him:

> *"I feared that in the midst of the dangers, difficulties and trials which would necessarily be connected with such a work, some who were comparatively inexperienced*

*Christians would break down, and bitterly reproach me for having encouraged them to undertake such an enterprise for which they were unequal ... On Sunday, June 25th 1865, unable to bear the sight of a congregation of a thousand or more Christian people rejoicing in their own security, while millions were perishing for lack of knowledge, I wandered out on the sands alone, in great spiritual agony; and there the Lord conquered my unbelief, and I surrendered myself to God for this service. I told him that all the responsibility as to issues and consequences must rest with him; that as his servant, it was mine to obey and to follow him—His, to direct, to care for, and to guide me **and those who might labour with me.**"*

Marshall Broomhall, Hudson Taylor:
The Man Who Believed God, page 117

Paul doesn't teach that everyone has to travel abroad as he did—indeed, he doesn't recruit these Elders to come with him. But Paul often writes of our individual and collective obligation to do whatever we can, as the people we are in the circumstances God has given us, to make disciples of all nations for Christ. De Young and Gilbert's excellent book *What is the Mission of the Church?* concludes, "The mission of the church, as seen in the Great Commissions, the early church in Acts, and the life of the Apostle Paul, is to win people to Christ and to build them up in Christ. Making disciples—that's our task."

In too many of our towns and cities, there is a tragedy unfolding with people from all nations drowning in sin, with disturbing parallels to the tragic loss of life when the huge luxury liner *Titanic* went down in 1912 off the coast of Newfoundland. The ship struck an iceberg and over 1,500 of the 2,200 passengers and crew drowned. The loss of life was greatly increased by four factors:

- There were insufficient lifeboats for the people—just as there are insufficient Bible-teaching churches in our towns and cities: we need to plant more.

- The poorer passengers were locked below decks while the wealthy boarded the lifeboats—just as the poorer communities of our towns and cities are often least served by gospel churches: we need to plant in the poorer communities.

- The crew of the ship were poorly trained in handling the lifeboats—just as our congregations are often poorly trained in evangelism: we need to train our membership not just in bringing people to church events but in personal evangelism.

- But most shocking of all... the half-empty lifeboats lacked the compassion to go back for the drowning—the saved too anxious to preserve their own safety to risk returning for the dying—just as many of our churches are half-full but care little for those all around them drowning in sin: we need to learn the compassion of Jesus.

When God became flesh in Jesus, he came as an evangelist, church-planter and cross-cultural missionary. When he began his public ministry, he called his disciples saying, "Follow me, and I will make you fishers of men" (Matthew 4:19, ESV)— and when leaving them, he said, "Go and make disciples of all nations" (28:19), and poured out his Spirit on his witnesses to take the gospel to the ends of the earth. To encourage us to persevere in his global mission despite persecution, he gave John a vision of a glorious feast in heaven, of "a great multitude that no one could count, from every nation, tribe, people and language, standing before the throne and before the Lamb"

(Revelation 7:9). For our risen Lord Jesus will accomplish his global mission, and invites us to join in the work.

Let us resolve that our churches will not be like cruise ships half-full of passengers dedicated to our own comfort, but lifeboats full of crew devoted to reaching all who are drowning without Jesus. Like Paul, may we learn from Jesus to be relentless in trying to reach *everywhere*, tell *everyone*, teach *everything* and take *every opportunity* to make disciples of all nations for Christ... for the glory of God alone.

Think it through

1. *To what extent does the Great Commission shape our priorities in life?*

2. *How could we get more involved, personally or with finance and prayer, in reaching "all nations" with the gospel—whether by cross-cultural evangelism, church-planting or global mission?*

3. *Who are you seeking to "disciple" at the moment and how?*

Church leaders: *How can you help establish the core mission of your church in making disciples of all nations for Christ?*

EXPOSITORY GUIDE TO
EPHESIANS

Richard Coekin helps readers see how being *"in Christ"* changes our view of ourselves, our world, our future, our churches and our workplaces. An eight-study *Good Book Guide* is also available for leading Ephesians in small groups.

ALSO AVAILABLE IN THE SERIES

thegoodbook.com/for-you   thegoodbook.co.uk/for-you

thegoodbook
COMPANY

Opening up the Bible

At The Good Book Company, we are dedicated to helping Christians and local churches grow. We believe that God's growth process always starts with hearing clearly what he has said to us through his timeless word—the Bible.

Ever since we opened our doors in 1991, we have been striving to produce resources that honour God in the way the Bible is used. We have grown to become an international provider of user-friendly resources to the Christian community, with believers of all backgrounds and denominations using our Bible studies, books, evangelistic resources, DVD-based courses and training events.

We want to equip ordinary Christians to live for Christ day by day, and churches to grow in their knowledge of God, their love for one another, and the effectiveness of their outreach.

Call us for a discussion of your needs or visit one of our local websites for more information on the resources and services we provide.

Your friends at The Good Book Company

NORTH AMERICA   thegoodbook.com   866 244 2165
UK & EUROPE   thegoodbook.co.uk   0333 123 0880
AUSTRALIA   thegoodbook.com.au   (02) 9564 3555
NEW ZEALAND   thegoodbook.co.nz   (+64) 3 343 2463

WWW.CHRISTIANITYEXPLORED.ORG
Our partner site is a great place for those exploring the Christian faith, with a clear explanation of the good news, powerful testimonies and answers to difficult questions.